faith
in the future

Books by Patrick Nachtigall

Available from Warner Press

Passport of Faith

Faith in the Future

faith
in the future
Christianity's Interface with Globalization

Patrick
Nachtigall

Warner Press
Anderson, Indiana

*This book is dedicated to Rev. Kermit Morrison
and Rev. Bill Martin (1929–2008), two great
pastors who had faith in my future.*

Coordinator of Publishing & Creative Services
Church of God Ministries, Inc.
PO Box 2420
Anderson, IN 46018-2420
800-848-2464
www.chog.org

To purchase additional copies of this book, to inquire about distribution, and for all other sales-related matters, please contact:

Warner Press, Inc.
PO Box 2499
Anderson, IN 46018-2499
800-741-7721
www.warnerpress.org

Cover and text design by Carolyn Frost
Edited by Stephen R. Lewis

ISBN-13: 978-1-59317-317-3

Library of Congress Cataloging-in-Publication Data

Nachtigall, Patrick, 1970-
    Faith in the future : Christianity's interface with globalization / Patrick Nachtigall.
        p.   cm.
    Includes bibliographical references.
    ISBN 978-1-59317-317-3 (pbk.)
    1. Globalization--Religious aspects--Christianity. I. Title.
    BR115.G59N33 2008
    261.09'0511--dc22   2008010963

Printed in the United States of America.

08 09 10 11 12 13/ VP / 10 9 8 7 6 5 4 3 2 1

contents

part II: the challenges

acknowledgements

ONCE AGAIN, I am thrilled to partner with the publishing team that produced this book, particularly Joe Allison. And Stephen Lewis is not only a great editor, but he has become a close friend and confidant who inspires me in my own faith.

I must also thank Dr. Bob Edwards for continuing to encourage me in my writing, speaking, and teaching. Bob's ability to offer wonderful Christian leadership to all of us on the mission field has been a true blessing, and his support of us will never be forgotten. Amanda Owens at *Missions* magazine has been a total delight to work with and I appreciate all of her support.

In Costa Rica, I would like to thank my father, Harry Nachtigall, who gave me a love for the church and an interest in the countries of the world that has remained with me to this day.

Here in Hong Kong, I must thank the brothers and sisters at the Hong Kong Church of God for all of their love and support. I am very proud of them, and it has been the thrill of a lifetime to do ministry with them. I also want to thank Dan Kelly for his friendship to our family and his support of my writing projects.

Last, but certainly not least, I want to thank my wonderful wife Jamie and my precious son Marco. Jamie's beauty, intelligence, talent, grace, and generosity continue to inspire me more and more every day, and I am so grateful that we have been able to see so much of this wonderful world together. My four-year-old son Marco's sweet, gentle spirit and sensitivity toward the things of God not only gives me hope for the future, it also humbles and inspires me to do my best for the Lord and the world he created. I am grateful that you are both in my life, and I look forward to experiencing these exciting times together.

introduction

Engage the World, Engage the Future!

*History unfolds itself by strange and
unpredictable paths. We have little control
over the future; and none at all over the past.*

Winston Churchill

ATTEMPTING TO PREDICT the future is never really a good idea. History is
riddled with the predictions of people who felt sure that they knew where
the future was headed and were later proved embarrassingly or tragically
wrong.

British Prime Minister Neville Chamberlain returned home from Hitler's
Germany in 1938 and predicted that the German dictator was a trustworthy
man and that the future would bring "peace for our time." A few short years
later, Hitler's name was synonymous with evil and Chamberlain's with appeasement and poor judgment. Religious leaders have not been much better
at predicting the future than politicians. They have often been pessimistic
about the future, incorrectly predicting impending doom and destruction.
Saint Martin of Tours, Pope Innocent III, Joseph Smith, William Miller, Herbert
W. Armstrong, Hal Lindsey, and even Billy Graham at one point all thought
that the end of the world was imminent, only to be proven wrong. Either God
regularly postpones the end of the world or the claims made in his name
about the future have been expressed with a bit too much certainty.

Throughout history, some have predicted a rosy future and others doom,
but there have always been people who have made the mistake of suggest-
ing that nothing unusual was occurring in the present, completely oblivious
to sweeping changes afoot that were radically reshaping the future. Horace
Rackham, visionary Henry Ford's lawyer, was told by the president of Michi-

gan Savings Bank, "The horse is here to stay, but the automobile is only a novelty—a fad." Ken Olson, president, chairman, and founder of Digital Equipment Corp., is famously quoted as saying, in 1977, "There is no reason anyone would want a computer in their home."

Other people see the changes occurring around them but underestimate the rate at which everything is being transformed. In 1949, *Popular Mechanics* predicted that computers would one day have only a thousand vacuum tubes and weigh no more than 1.5 tons, which was indeed better than the thirty-ton computers of the day but obviously way off the mark. *Newsweek* magazine, which today worries about climate change, predicted in the 1960s that safaris in Vietnam would be the great tourism experience of the decade. Needless to say, things in Vietnam were changing far more quickly than was thought, but for the worse. At one point in the 1970s, both overpopulation and global cooling were of great concern, but the reality was that birthrates were starting to decline dramatically in most industrial countries and apparently the world was actually getting hotter in that decade.

If history has taught us anything, it is that the future is impossible to predict and that it always takes strange and unpredictable turns. At the end of the nineteenth century, nobody would have predicted World War I, World War II, the invention of nuclear weapons, the cold war, the rise and fall of the Berlin Wall, or the end of China's empire and its journey to capitalism by way of Marxism. These are just a few of the major world-turning events that took everyone by surprise. To think that we can now peer into the proverbial crystal ball and accurately predict the future would be folly of the greatest order. This new century will surprise us.

In this book, I do not make bold claims about the future (okay, maybe a few), but ultimately, my purpose is not to try and predict what *will* happen. I am at least reasonable enough to say that I do not possess that kind of knowledge. I do, however, want to look at some of the new things that are *currently* happening in our world so that Christians can be better informed and more prepared to engage the world with the gospel. Change is in the air and we must be alert.

New Challenges and Opportunities for Christians

I do believe that we can safely say that since the end of the cold war in 1991, we have entered into a unique period of history. The world is undergoing a process of what I call *hyper*globalization. As I argued in my book *Passport of Faith: A Christian's Encounter with World Religions*, globalization has always been occurring to some extent throughout history. However, the speed and scale of today's cultural, technological, political, and economic globalization is so great that only two other eras in history are remotely comparable: the Age of Discovery, beginning in 1492 with Columbus, and the Industrial Revolution, which flourished in the nineteenth century.[1] The new technological innovations and the intense global interaction that is occurring today is creating new opportunities and new challenges at a tremendous pace. It is impossible to forecast what our societies will look like at the end of the twenty-first century, but we can piece together a picture of the opportunities and challenges.

A platform is being built right now, and even though we do not know what the structure will look like when finished, we can at least examine the materials and technology being used to create the structure. Already, there are new opportunities that we Christians can seize in this new era, such as the spread of the gospel through new forms of technology.

Technology is value neutral and can be used for both good and bad. In China, I met young people that had seen the previews for Mel Gibson's *The Passion of the Christ* on their computers before the film was in theaters in the West. Within months, these young people were able to easily obtain bootleg copies of the entire film. Only a few years earlier, trying to sneak the Christian message or even a Bible into China would have been difficult. Today, there is more information flowing into closed countries than can be processed by authorities hostile to Christianity. This is providing Christians with new opportunities and exposing more people to the gospel than ever before. This is clearly a good thing. But DVD piracy, theft, and the criminal networks that are forming and taking advantage of this new technology are bad.

---

1. Dates for the Industrial Revolution vary widely from historian to historian. The changes began in the eighteenth century, but it was not until the early nineteenth century that the revolution truly flourished, leading to widespread change. In fact, the mid-nineteenth century is identified as the beginning of the Second Industrial Revolution with the rise of steam power, internal combustion engines, and electrical power generation.

Or take the case of the cell phone in Africa. Many villages that were cut-off from the world by bad roads only a couple of years ago now have cell-phone base stations nearby, transforming individual lives and the economies of many African nations. Cell phones not only help African entrepreneurs, but they have also become a way for Africans to transfer money over long distances. The cell phone is making African economies more efficient, and that is not simply a matter of making more money. The implications go far beyond cash to opening up possibilities for a new generation.

But cell phones have a darker side. They are indispensable to criminal groups because they make organization and planning easier. They have been particularly useful for drug runners and terrorists, as well as for criminal networks involved in the global sex slave trade. With cell phones, there is no need for a fixed base, numbers can be changed quickly and frequently, and phones can be thrown away immediately after use to avoid detection.

Another problem with cell phones is that they require a metal called coltan, which is mined in Africa, the very continent that is being transformed in positive ways by cell-phone technology. The demand for coltan, though, means that many mines in Africa are now crewed by children who dig through the dirt for twelve or more hours a day. Rarely do these children receive pay for their efforts, and if they do, they may be robbed on their way home of the little they have earned for their backbreaking labor. This is the price of using cell phones. One of these young African boys who was interviewed by the BBC said that his hope is to one day escape the coltan mines to become a pastor. How heartbreaking!

New ways to help the world are being created everyday, yet new humanitarian challenges are opening up as well. The growth of democracy, the World Wide Web, and the rapid expansion of the global economy are all bringing both good and evil on a large scale. In this new age, even the smallest, cheapest things can have incredible uses both for the betterment of humanity and for its exploitation.

Engage the World!

Good and evil have always coexisted on the planet, but there are so many new opportunities and challenges arising in this new era that it is worth cultivating the habit of mind that examines new developments from a Christian perspective. This book aims to help us develop that habit of mind. There are no easy answers in this book to the serious problems that are emerging, but the first step is to inform ourselves about the world, and the second step is to commit ourselves to engaging the world as Christians. Perhaps this book will awaken the global activist in all of us. That is my hope.

In Part I, I highlight some of the exciting and encouraging trends and opportunities that globalization is bringing to us; in Part II, I focus on some of the disturbing, disruptive challenges we face. I hope to offer a quick overview of where we stand at this moment in history and to highlight some of the areas where Christians can make a difference.

Globalization encompasses many different issues, consequently there are many key areas not addressed in this book but which are equally important: these include bioethics, refugee crises, failed states, pandemics, and immigration. For a basic introduction on globalization, I recommend reading "7 Questions Regarding Globalization," which can be found in the appendix of this book.

Jesus told us to not to be consumed with worry over the days to come. When he said this, however, I do not believe that he was saying that we should avoid thinking critically about the issues of our day and just live moment to moment oblivious to the changes occurring around us. Jesus was a forward thinker who chose disciples, showed them how to do ministry, and sent them out to engage the world. His actions were deliberate as he consciously moved toward a future that would demand the ultimate submission and sacrifice from himself. Throughout it all, he modeled God's love for future generations and for the church, which, after his death and resurrection, became the most powerful force in shaping human history. Jesus obviously understood that we all need to think about our future to an extent. That is the reality of this life.

Instead, Jesus was warning us not be consumed by our own selfish concerns and desires. Today, Jesus still asks us not to worry about ourselves but to think of those around us, become disciples, and engage this world. Jesus had a plan for the future of God's people, and we are those people and this is our time. "It is not for you to know the times or dates the Father has set by his own authority. But you will receive power when the Holy Spirit comes on you; and you will be my witnesses in Jerusalem, and in all Judea and Samaria, and to the ends of the earth" (Acts 1:7–8).

Christianity is a powerful force for good, and we need to take that seriously. In this era of sweeping economic changes and tectonic social shifts, what we say about our beliefs will be a lot less important to people than our actions and the way we actually live our lives. As we present Christianity to this fallen "brave new world," let us make sure that we Christians are not simply known for talking about the differences between Christianity and other religions; let us actually go into the world and *make a difference*.

part I
the opportunities

1

how the world
got its groove back

An unprecedented era of peace is upon us.

*It's better to be a dog in a peaceful time than
be a man in a chaotic period.*

Chinese Proverb

EVERY PERSON READING these words today is fortunate to be alive in the safest, most prosperous, most peaceful era in human history. Even if you are carrying this book into a hot tin shack in the dusty slums of one of the world's poorest cities, life has never been better. Yes, many people are still living in terrible poverty and the world continues to suffer from violence and war, but the average human being today has a greater chance than ever before of dying a natural death, avoiding the experience of war, and making a decent living.

This is not delusional thinking; it is fact. For most of history, human life has been "solitary, poor, nasty, brutish and short,"[1] to quote the English philosopher Thomas Hobbes, who lived not that long ago in the very unpleasant seventeenth century. Even well into the twentieth century, enormous swaths of the globe were awash in poverty and violence. From Cambodia to England, most countries failed to escape the twentieth century without experiencing brutal war and poverty for some, if not all, of those one hundred years. But at the end of the twentieth century, we had reached some sort of turning point, and most have at least received a short reprieve from the chaos and anarchy that has characterized much of human history up to this point. Why has the world suddenly gotten safer and wealthier in recent decades? How did we

---

1. Thomas Hobbes, *Leviathan* (Andrew Crooke, 1651), xiii.

enter into this uniquely prosperous and peaceful moment in history? Wasn't the twentieth century filled with violence, war, and famine?

The Last Turning Point: Stumbling Towards Peace

The twentieth century was the most violent in human history[2], a century that saw two world wars and the invention of nuclear weaponry. After the detonation of the atomic bomb by the Americans brought World War II to an end, the rest of the world's most powerful nations also developed nuclear capabilities.

With these powerful new weapons, the stakes were so high that countries with nuclear capability had to avoid fighting each other directly. Instead, they began creating peace-minded economic and political alliances. This was a key marker in global history: the point at which the world's most powerful players had to *avoid* large-scale wars instead of waging them. This shift toward economic competition instead of military competition began the slow process of ushering in a new, less violent, more prosperous era. Of course, there was still the danger of thousands of nuclear missiles pointed at each other as the cold war ensued between the Soviets, the Chinese, and the West, but large-scale state-on-state warfare was avoided. This in turn opened the door for global capitalism to raise living standards.

This new, less volatile world of the rich and powerful nations of the globe often left out the underdeveloped third world or, worse yet, involved them in proxy wars as the world divided itself between East and West. The most famous of these harmful proxy wars was the Vietnam War, which ended in defeat for the United States and decades of poverty and oppression for Vietnam.

But in the past sixty years or so, many of these poorer, down-trodden countries achieved independence, and with the end of the cold war they have experienced dramatic declines in regional conflict and exponential growth of incomes. Today's level of peace, prosperity, and international cooperation is unprecedented in human history.

---

2. The twentieth century was the most violent in terms of the number of people killed, not in the number of battles and day-to-day wars, which were far greater in the centuries before nation-states were established.

Of course, there are still wars and people living in poverty. The Iraq war is in the news daily, as is the suffering and poverty of the refugees in Darfur, Sudan. These are obviously tragic exceptions. But not only are there far fewer countries at war, there are entire regions that are peaceful now. Twenty years ago, traveling through much of Latin America, Asia, and sub-Saharan Africa for leisure would have been tantamount to suicide. Today, many of the countries once associated with war and violence are peaceful enough to be developing tourism industries. The Ho Chi Minh Trail in Vietnam, which was once used to transport machines for killing, is now lined with golf courses for tourists.

The impending racial explosion in South Africa never materialized; instead, not only is it Africa's brightest economic spot, but its multiracial leadership has become a diplomatic force for peace throughout the African continent. Even previously violent Colombia is seeing change as a democratically elected president (one of Latin America's many democratically elected leaders now) clamps down on narco-traffickers and their militias, bringing widespread peace and economic resurgence to booming cities like Cali and Bogotá.

Today's level of peace, prosperity, and international cooperation is unprecedented in human history.

The greatest weapon in history set the stage for a new, more peaceful era in which peace and interconnectivity have became indispensable to economic success. Great nations had to downsize large-scale wars or risk losing everything. Thus the events of 1945 had implications far greater than anyone could have predicted at the time. The big war of the future was "cold" instead of hot, and the smaller hot wars, while destructive, never escalated to the point of using nuclear weapons. Things got very dangerous before they got better (the Cuban missile crisis comes to mind). But ultimately, the cold war ended with the fall of the Berlin Wall and the collapse of the Soviet Union, and that in turn brought an end to the proxy wars in Latin America, Africa, and Southeast Asia. The remaining powerful ideological enemy of the West, China, chose McDonald's and capitalism over Karl Marx, and the rest is history—only kinder, gentler, and more peaceful. Thomas Hobbes would be shocked. Instead of lives that are "solitary, poor, nasty, brutish and short," increasingly the majority of the world's citizens are living lives that are interdependent, prosperous, comfortable, civilized, and long.

The Disappearance of the "Third World"?

I believe that we may have now reached another milestone that will set the course for this next stage of history, just as the use of the atomic bomb did in the previous century. As in the cold war era, there will be times in this new era that will be very dangerous; but in the long run, it may also ultimately lead to many good things. What is this marker that is upon us? It is the fact that many of the so-called third-world nations of the past are now developing economically at a rate that is so great that large segments of their populations are catching up to the rich countries of the developed first world.

The disappearance of many third-world nations (to be replaced by newly emerging nations, with a huge divide between rich and poor *within* the countries) characterizes this new century. According to the September 14, 2006, edition of *The Economist*, the combined output of emerging economies now accounts for more than half of the total world gross domestic product (GDP). Instead of living in a world where only one-third of the nations produce any kind of significant economic output, we are quickly moving toward a world where the vast majority of citizens will be living in interconnected countries generating wealth. The ramifications of this are enormous. The third world, as we have known it, is disappearing.

The term *third world* has been in decline in recent years due to the fact that it was originally a cold war term that referred to nations aligned with neither the West (the first world) nor the less developed but militarily powerful Communist sphere (the second world). It has remained a helpful term because so many people understand it. Recently, the term has also become politically incorrect and is often discarded in favor of terms such as the *Global South*, the *two-thirds world*, and the *majority world*. But increasingly, those terms do not make sense either, since many underdeveloped nations are not in the South and *two-thirds* and *majority* do not really represent what is occurring economically.

> Much of the third world is interconnecting with the first world.

What is happening is that many underdeveloped countries and countries with large numbers of poor people are raising living standards rapidly, and pockets of their populations are highly plugged into the first world. In this book, I will use the term *emerging nations* for those newly interconnected nations and *least developed countries* (LDCs) for those that remain discon-nected and mired in widespread poverty. First-world nations will be referred to as *developed nations*.

The two most obvious examples of emerging nations are India and China, two countries whose names were equated with third-world poverty for most of the twentieth century. Even people unfamiliar with Chinese history and global affairs knew that China was a place of great famines—the kind of place where people ate tree bark and drank horse urine to survive. "Eat your veg-etables, because there are people starving in China!" we were told as children. And India fared no better in people's minds, associated as it was with images of filth and disease. The global symbol of caring for the world's poor was Mother Teresa, who served the sick and dying on the streets of Calcutta.

But today, China is the fourth largest economy in the world. And while Chi-na's economy is still far, far behind that of the United States, it is the economy having the greatest impact globally, whether through the economic boom it is giving fully developed nations like Australia, the cheap goods it provides for America, or the infrastructure and loans it provides in least developed countries in Africa and Latin America. Meanwhile, India now has its own high-tech industries, its fair share of billionaires, and its own Silicon Valleys. Even in Mother Teresa's home of Calcutta (now renamed Kolkata), there are now fancy hotels and luxurious shopping malls as the city rebrands itself as the "Eastern gateway to India."

The rise of India and China has received a lot of press, but the story goes far beyond India and China. Beyond those two countries, other emerging nations scattered throughout the world, countries like Vietnam, Malaysia, Uruguay, Ireland, and Estonia—places rarely thought about—are becoming players in the global economy. Much of the third world is interconnecting with the first world. The resulting transformations mean that our geopolitical definitions need to be redefined.

Good News from Africa?

While the developed nations (first world) have been focusing on emerging nations China and India, countries in Europe, Latin America, and the rest of Asia are rising as well. Africa and the Middle East, however, remain a source of concern. But even here there is good news. Kenya has one of the fastest growing stock markets in the world, as does Egypt. Both countries are in regions that have severely underperformed economically, yet even in these traditionally economic backwaters, there are signs of hope. For five straight years, growth in sub-Saharan Africa (traditionally the world's most underperforming region economically) has expanded by a rate of more than 5 percent for five years in a row. The percentage is expected to grow in 2008.[3]

Yes, Africa is still a poverty-stricken region with an average annual income per capita of $600 and three hundred million living in poverty.[4] But things are changing rapidly in many of these countries that were once awash in war, disease, and economic stagnation. In the democracy of Ghana, the economy is growing by 6 percent a year and the national debt is down by two-thirds. Foreign investors have taken note that returns can be 20 percent higher in Ghana than anywhere else, and there are now middle-class neighborhoods in Accra and some four-bedroom homes cost $500,000.[5]

Liberia, which in recent years has been recovering from two devastating civil wars, is an example of a least developed country that continued suffering even after the cold war ended. It has proven difficult to govern, but today, it is led by a Harvard-educated woman who is trying to end the cycle of poverty and war. While Liberia has a long way to go, the changes that this democratically elected female president has ushered in are already significant.

> **Al Jazeera is causing many Muslims to ask, "Why can't we have those freedoms?"**

At the other end of the spectrum is Botswana, which is rarely in the news. Not only is Botswana one of Africa's most livable places, but it has intelligently decreased its economic dependence on mineral wealth and allowed foreign companies to set up shop and benefit from its low corporate tax rate. In 2004, Botswana was ranked as one of the least corrupt nations in the world by Transparency International

---

3. Chris Thomlinson, "Ghana Reflects Progress in Africa," *Washington Post*, December 2, 2007, http://www.washingtonpost.com/wp-dyn/content/article/2007/12/02/AR2007120201092.html.

4. Editorial, "Africa's Chance," *New York Times*, http://www.nytimes.com/2007/11/02/opinion/02fri1.html?_r=1&oref=slogin. According to the United Nations Environment Programme, this number refers to people living on less than $1.50 per day and without access to basic sanitation and hygiene.

5. Thomlinson, "Ghana Reflects Progress in Africa."

ahead of many countries in Asia and Europe. In 2005, Standard & Poor's gave it a sovereign credit rating of A, designating it as one of the safest places in the world to invest.

In the past couple of years, Africa has seen its GDP grow faster than at any time in the past twenty years, and sixteen countries in sub-Saharan Africa have favorable credit ratings.[6] This is not the image of Africa that most of us have in our head. Africans are slowly changing their opinion of themselves as well. In a recent Pew Global Attitudes survey, nine out of ten African countries surveyed believed their lives would be better five years into the future.[7] Of course, similar high hopes surrounded the continent in the 1960s and ultimately ended in disappointment, but we should not discount Africa at this time. Some fundamental changes are starting to occur in key areas, most notably, some very resourceful, entrepreneurial innovation.

Islamic Nations: Al Qaeda or Al Jazeera?

Meanwhile, in the Middle East, where poverty, illiteracy, and economic growth levels often approach sub-Saharan African levels, the tiny Middle Eastern country of the United Arab Emirates now has one-fifth of the world's construction cranes on its construction sites and grandiose projects that rival those of China. The U.A.E. does not want to rely only on oil for its economic future; this is a very smart and progressive move for this region, which has allowed its development to languish, choosing to depend solely on oil wealth. The U.A.E. is now venturing into other areas, including tourism, high-tech industry, and the creation of a services economy, to generate future income and growth for the country.

Forty years ago, this desert land was poverty-stricken, had worms in the drinking water, and no electricity. Today, Dubai has become a futuristic city in the middle of the desert—a high-tech version of Las Vegas (without the gambling, of course). Dubai now boasts the world's most luxurious hotel, the tallest building in the world (known as Burj Dubai), the largest mall in the world, and The World itself. The World is an archipelago of large luxury

---

6. Jennifer Brea, "Africans to Bono: 'For God's Sake Please Stop!', *The American*, July 3, 2007, http://www.american.com/archive/2007/july-0707/africans-to-bono-for-gods-sake-please-stop.

7. Thomlinson, "Ghana Reflects Progress in Africa."

housing developments built on islands of sand reclaimed from the Persian Gulf that resemble the shapes of countries on a map. The U.A.E. also has one of the world's best airlines, Emirates, based out of the new Dubai International Airport, which now serves as a key link between Europe and Asia and will soon become a global connecting point offering direct flights from six continents. Furthermore, the U.A.E. has freedoms that other countries in the region do not have, such as property rights for foreigners and the freedom to attend Christian churches.

Both Qatar and Saudi Arabia are trying to copy Dubai's success. The latter is particularly encouraging since the nineteen hijackers that attacked the United States on September 11, 2001, came from Saudi Arabia. Meanwhile, Islamic terrorism and interest in al Qaeda is temporarily on the wane throughout the region. The overwhelming majority of terrorist incidents since September 11, 2001, have taken place as part of the Iraq war. Throughout the Middle East, the brutalities and futility of war are being televised as are the benefits of peace and prosperity.

In the Persian Gulf country of Qatar, the city of Doha is home to the twenty-four-hour Arab-based news channel Al Jazeera, which also broadcasts an English version globally. Criticized as a propaganda tool against the West, Al Jazeera is actually doing something the West can only applaud: It is televising images of places like United Arab Emirates, Qatar, and the rest of the rapidly developing Islamic world to those nations still ruled by repressive Islamic leaders. In other words, Al Jazeera is providing Muslims with a window into the emerging nations

> A loss of Chinese goods in American stores would actually increase poverty in the United States.

and causing many to ask, "Why can't we have those freedoms?" The globalization of Arab news is a good thing, creating a hunger for freedom and opportunity.

Turkey is a secular state that has seen a renewed interest in Islam and the strengthening of the Islamic political party. Nevertheless, Turkey is highly progressive and boasts an economy that is one of the largest and fastest-growing in the world. Thus far, Islamic political gains have not translated into hostility or ruinous economic policies as they did in Iran after the revolution of 1979.

In Asia, the tiny Islamic sultanate of Brunei is also trying to open up to the world. Brunei is located on the island of Borneo, which conjures up images of dense jungles, headhunters, and exotic wildlife. Borneo is still an untamed place and home to one of the largest caves in the world, which houses more than three million bats. Nevertheless, change is afoot here as well. In 2007, I visited the capital city of Bandar Seri Begawan, which is very small and still has a large population of people living along the river in homes on stilts. People have been living in these stilt homes on the jungle river for hundreds of years. Yet just beyond those stilt homes, in the heart of the very small downtown district, is Microsoft Corporation's Brunei headquarters. The Redmond, Washington–based company has an office amid the jungles and stilt-homes of Borneo. Places like Borneo that in the past have been totally disconnected from the developed nations are now constantly interacting with that world and are seeing their countries transform more rapidly than at any time in history.

The Key: Greater Openness and Interconnectivity

With more competition and more minds around the world innovating and sharing information on everything from computers to medical technology, we will probably see new revolutionary breakthroughs in many different fields. For instance, Andy Kessler predicts in his intriguing book *The End of Medicine* that we may very well experience a shift from treating most illnesses at the hospital to preventing them altogether—in our own homes. These kinds of radical breakthroughs will not just be generated by one country (the United States) from one area of highly concentrated competitors (Silicon Valley) but from many Silicon Valleys scattered throughout the world in such unlikely places as Chennai, India; Doha, Qatar; Dublin, Ireland; and Wuhan, China. These places already exist. The developed nations are no longer the only places where good things happen, where living standards are high, and where rich people live. In this new world, many emerging nations will have the chance to compete and reap the profits of greater opportunities, more wealth, and higher living standards.

Although globalization is about economic development, it is not *just* about raw economics. It is about openness and interconnectivity—culturally, politically, economically, socially, and spiritually. The level of global

how the world got its groove back ⁘ **17**

interconnectivity means that countries at odds with each other (like Taiwan and China) may no longer have the luxury of antagonizing each other. Too many Chinese companies are supported by Taiwanese investors (and too many Chinese men are marrying Taiwanese women) for them to be enemies. War is becoming more expensive, not just in terms of military hardware, but in terms of its effects on national economies. South Korea and Japan may still have hostile feelings toward each other, but can they afford to go to war when they are so interdependent economically? While it is true that history has seen large powers go to war even when the costs greatly outweighed the benefits, we must remember that many of these emerging nations, such as China and Russia, have just left an era of chaos and devastation caused by war and they are not eager to repeat the experience.

The same equation applies to new rivalries, such as that between the United States and China. Both countries are making billions of dollars off of each other each year in a win-win game (contrary to what politicians tell us in order to get elected). A loss of Chinese goods in American stores would actually increase poverty in the United States because the price of everything from underwear to computers would go up; the buying power of the American consumer would drop. An American woman recently wrote a book documenting her attempt to live for a year without using any goods made in China.[8] It was nearly impossible. What she discovered was that U.S. trade with China makes things in America more affordable and life better. For example, tennis shoes for her children would cost $15 if made in China and sold at Payless; Italian-made tennis shoes cost $65. In myriad ways, she had more options and saved more money by using Chinese goods. Without them, her life became very difficult. Even brewing her necessary daily cup of coffee with her Chinese-made coffee-maker had to be abandoned.

Of all people, Christians should fear globalization the least!

Many things that we use every day are not made in the United States, and they never will be again because we are primarily a service-oriented economy

---

8. Sara Bongiorni, *A Year Without "Made in China": One Family's True Life Adventure in the Global Economy* (Hoboken, NJ: John Wiley & Sons, 2007).

with under 10 percent of our economy comprised of manufacturing and farming. It is for this reason that we, as a developed nation, are so wealthy. Returning to a primarily agricultural and manufacturing existence is impossible at this point, which is why we need China, India, and Mexico. Their economies are still heavily rooted in agriculture and manufacturing and will be for years to come. Furthermore, even if the label reads "Made in China," the product may very well have been outsourced to Bangladesh by an American-owned factory in Shanghai. These labels mean very little anymore.

One of the grand ironies in this new era is that after decades of fighting Marxist socialism in the cold war, Americans are suddenly crying uncle: these former countries have turned to free-market capitalism just as we always wanted, but now we feel that they are providing too much competition. Talk about wanting to have your cake and eat it too! At this point, China, Russia, Vietnam and all of the rest of our former enemies are more than a century away from being able to match the per capita household wealth of the United States. Few of us will be alive when that day arrives.

The United States has always feared any kind of competition. After Western Europe was decimated by World War II, Americans feared that rebuilding Europe would hurt our economy. The same was true in the 1970s in response to the proposed creation of the European Union. And in the 1980s, Japan was the key economic and military competitor that was supposedly going to overtake America. In reality, when nations remain open to each other and increase interconnectivity, living standards increase across the board. An economically stronger China will lead to an economically stronger America. It will also lead to a more open, freer China.

And then there are those parts of the world, like the Democratic Republic of Congo, a least developed country, which have long been ignored by Europe and the United States. Congo (DR) is now getting a new opportunity to jump start its economy because of Chinese investment in African infrastructure. As the emerging nation of China hunts for natural resources to maintain its rapid development, LDCs in Africa and Latin America are benefiting. Chinese investment means new schools, hospitals, and jobs. China has been accused of recolonizing Africa and exploiting the continent; while that may be the case at times, China is also learning very rapidly that in this age of twenty-four-hour news, an interconnected country has to care about the people it is working with, not simply exploit them for resources. While China is under pressure to be more socially and environmentally conscientious, the same openness and interconnectivity is also exerting positive pressure on Africa and Latin America to create successful institutions that support these new investments.

The openness of social interaction is also affecting places that were once homogenous and that interacted very little with the outside world. As recently as the early 1990s, Ireland was still primarily poor and monocultural, with many people emigrating elsewhere to find better jobs and opportunities. Today, Ireland is Europe's fastest-growing economy and thronged with Polish and Lithuanian immigrants. Places like Ireland that were once only exposed to one race or one culture are now becoming global in nature. Toronto is the world's most multicultural city, surpassing even New York. Melbourne, Australia, has the second largest Greek population outside of Athens. Around the world from Houston to Sydney, a generation of young people is growing up accustomed to interacting with people from different cultures. From Iowa to Auckland, the rise of Thai restaurants is just one sign that the world is moving into our neighborhoods. The vast majority of us are benefiting from this and enjoying it.

This in turn is opening the door to spiritual interaction. A Korean that has moved to the United States is nine times more likely to become a Christian than one in South Korea. While celebrities dabble in Jewish Kabala and the occasional European converts to Buddhism, the big winner in all of this cultural interaction is Christianity, which is seeing spectacular growth across cultures and in the unlikeliest of places. Not only is globalization good for the global economy, but it is absolutely fantastic for Christianity. It presents the Christian church with a golden opportunity to reduce poverty, educate people, enter countries that were once closed, and witness the explosion of Christianity into new cultures. Of all people, Christians should fear globalization the least! It is literally bringing the world to our doorstep and giving us the opportunity to share Christ on an unprecedented scale. I believe Christ would tell us not to be afraid of these changes but rather to embrace them.

What about the Downsides?

Two-thirds of the world's countries are now seeing their standards of living and economic lot improve more dramatically than ever before. Many countries that have been referred to as third-world countries until recently now play a key role in the global economy, have a rapidly growing middle class, and have regions where living standards are similar to developed nations. I have visited many of these countries repeatedly over the past couple of decades and have seen firsthand the progress occurring in these nations. It is abundantly clear to me that these dramatic changes are happening.

Of course, there are problems in the development process; these will be explored further in Part II of this book. Globalization ushers in a lot of rapid change, and the current spirit of goodwill between nations will be tested. Within each country, there will be tensions as well, and we may be entering an era in which turmoil *within* nations is more dangerous than turmoil between nations. The Vegas-like creations of Dubai are being built on the backs of poor Asian migrants, often unfairly paid. Kenya still suffers from too much tribalism, as the 2007 presidential elections demonstrated, which hinders its social and economic progress. Egypt has an urbanization problem: far too many poor are living in the slums of Cairo. These are glimpses of the challenges that will face us on a larger scale in the future. Overall, contrary to doomsayers and apocalyptic fundamentalists, things have never been better. But even when things are very good, the bad still takes center stage. In this new age of 24/7 global media, perception will often mean more than reality.

> **In this new age of 24/7 global media, perception will often mean more than reality.**

For many, globalization is a scary word, conjuring up images of losing one's job and homogenization of the world's cultures and diversity into one global culture controlled by large corporations. In the West, we fear a world where everyone loses their job to some worker in an emerging nation, while in emerging nations, people fear a world dominated by American culture. But is this what is happening under globalization? Not really.

Take the issue of job outsourcing. It is true that many call centers have been moved to places like India and that automotive jobs have been moved to Mexico. This has certainly been hard on those regions, such as the American Midwest, that are heavily dependent on that kind of industry. What is often ignored, though, is the fact that very few people lose their jobs because a company has moved them overseas. In 2004, at the height of the off-shoring fears, 1.9 percent of layoffs in the United States were due to overseas relocation.[9] The worst-case scenario is that 3.3 million U.S. jobs would be outsourced over fifteen years; on an annual basis, this would ultimately affect less than 0.2 percent of employed Americans.[10]

More importantly, emerging nations like India and China that are perceived to be a threat to U.S. jobs are actually creating more jobs in the United States than they are eliminating. Indian companies like Infosys now hire U.S. college students, train them in India, and send them back to offices in the United States. The Indian company Wipro is opening a software center in Atlanta that will create five hundred jobs. Tata Consulting Services has opened an office in Phoenix, as well as in China, Brazil, Chile, and Uruguay, employing more than five thousand people outside of India.[11] A Chinese firm has recently built auto plants in Mississippi. Many of these Indian and Chinese companies provide jobs that otherwise would not exist. These investments even extend to least developed countries like Ethiopia, where the Chinese have recently opened an auto plant producing inexpensive cars for the African consumer.

Another point that is often overlooked is that 80 percent of the money made from manufacturing in China ends up in the hands of Western companies, since they are the ones setting up the plants. The result is the expansion of these companies and more jobs created in Western countries.

The reality is that off-shoring is often inconvenient and not worth the hassle for most companies, no matter which country they call home. The bulk of the economic challenges that developed nations face are internal issues, such as the high cost of U.S. health care, the government pork projects that have supported rural Japan, and the high tax rate in Denmark, which has caused workers to leave for greener pastures elsewhere. In other words, the wealthy developed nations of the world need to set their own houses in order, reducing debt and raising standards of education for a fast-moving high-tech

---

9. U.S. Government Accountability Office, *International Trade: Current Government Data Provide Limited Insight into Offshoring of Services* (Washington, DC: U.S. Government Accountability Office, 2004), 34. http://www.gao.gov/new.items/d04932.pdf

10. Daniel W. Drezner, "The Outsourcing Bogeyman," *Foreign Affairs,* May–June 2004: 83. http://www.foreignaffairs.org/20040501faessay83301/daniel-w-drezner/the-outsourcing-bogeyman.html

11. Anand Giridharadas, "Outsourcing Works, So India Is Exporting Jobs," *New York Times*, September 25, 2007. http://www.nytimes.com/2007/09/25/business/worldbusiness/25outsource.html?_r=2&oref=slogin&oref=slogin

world, instead of biting the hands that are not only feeding them but allowing them to buy big houses on credit. Globalization is providing great opportunities for countries like the United States, but developed nations are choosing to live recklessly rather than becoming fiscally responsible. Emerging nations provide a much better scapegoat for politicians from Washington to Berlin unwilling to deal with the politically tough issues at home.

As for the criticism that the world will succumb to American or Western culture, this does not seem to be the case either. Throughout the world, people are sipping chai, eating Thai, and watching Sky. Korean music and films are all the rage in Asia, while India's Bollywood and Hollywood are involved in joint productions. High-end Chinese designer brands are entering the market, and everyone's shaking their hips to the music of Colombian singer Shakira. Globalization actually seems to be encouraging cultural diversity and revealing its beauty.

Globalization seems to encourage cultural diversity and reveal its beauty.

As I wrote in my first book, *Passport of Faith*, the antiglobalization movement in the West is currently an incoherent hodgepodge of groups consisting of environmentalists, neo-Marxists, and labor activists who paint in broad strokes and have a poor understanding of economics and global cultures. They fail to see that it is technology, more than corporations, that is revolutionizing the world, and technology is not a genie that you can put back in the bottle. It benefits too many beyond just large corporations. A job lost in the American Midwest or in England's Midlands is probably due to the adoption of new technologies rather than off-shoring. And while capitalism and democracy can both be distasteful and damaging at times, none of these angry groups have come up with a macroeconomic model to replace the current global system. Marxism didn't turn out too well in the last century, and the countries with the most recent experience under planned centralized economies are the ones liberalizing the fastest.

Globalization is often counterintuitive. In Hong Kong, where I live, the great fear was that the city would be stifled and ruined once it reverted to Chinese control. Instead, China has become more like Hong Kong due to China's increasing interconnectivity with the rest of the world. The second great fear was that the city would be inundated with cheap workers from the mainland. But those workers found Hong Kong to be too expensive, and besides, there were plenty of new opportunities opening up at home. Then the antiglobalization movement targeted the sweatshops that employed these laborers, arguing that they were being exploited in factories. Chinese factories had to raise their standards to appease Western human rights groups and also because the migrant workers had so many factories to choose from. The next great fear was that migration to coastal cities like Shenzen, Shanghai, and Beijing would create a labor shortage in the interior. Instead, those very cities are experiencing a labor shortage because so many opportunities have been created closer to home.

Globalization creates options and flexibility and is often counterintuitive. Antiglobalization arguments are seldom rooted in reality. Globalization continues to throw us curve balls, but overwhelmingly more people win than lose.

In 2007, a lack of quality control by Chinese manufacturers was exposed with the discovery of toys coated with lead paint and pet food laced with poison, all exported from China. The Chinese found themselves in a panic, instituting an international public relations campaign to counter the negative publicity. Of note is the fact that the initial complaints about tainted Chinese exports came from the tiny country of Panama. This is significant because it shows that China and its government, once authoritarian and sealed off from the rest of the world, is now accountable, not only to Chinese citizens, but even to the citizens of Panama! Globalization creates new rules and forces even authoritarian China to hide the truth less and care more about the global community.

The strongest antiglobalization force thus far has been Islamic militants, particularly Osama bin Laden. His religious ideology is the opposite of that moment reported in Acts 2 when the Holy Spirit empowered diverse people gathered together from many cultures. Islamic militants attacked the World Trade Center, not once, but twice, and employees of more than eighty different nationalities lost their lives. The irony, of course, is that al Qaeda itself is a global movement with a loose structure that would be at home in Silicon Valley. These kinds of ironies seem to be missed by many of the opponents of globalization. The mobilization of antiglobalization activists is made possible by globalization itself.

Global capitalism is not Christianity, and we should never forget that. But a system that allows and rewards diversity, freedom, and choice is much better than one that tries to stifle creativity, variety, and the human spirit, as Marxism and Islamic fascism have done so easily in the past.[12]

Western Christians need to begin looking at globalization with a new understanding of key words in our vocabulary, words such as *interconnectivity*, *openness*, *freedom*, and *opportunity*. We need to admit that Western capitalism is not perfect. Capitalism can enslave people just as well as Marxism. A Russian from the Soviet Union once visited New York City and saw all the advertisements and said, "Wow! I thought our propaganda was bad." There's truth in that statement. The difference is that there is more choice and more flexibility in an open world than in a closed one. We must also remember that we in the West have lived for

> The mobilization of antiglobalization activists depends on globalization itself.

a long time in cities with excellent sanitation and in societies that provide schools for our children and roofs over our heads. The West has already spent decades living in tremendous luxury. Is it fair for us to be dismayed or angry that the rest of the world would like to experience improved standards of living and more opportunities for their children?

As Christians who are serious about obeying the command to take the gospel to the world, how can we not rejoice in the fact that not only is the world more open than ever before, but the world is even coming to our doorstep. We can easily reach out and touch the Samaritan woman at the well, and the Roman Centurion can easily find us when he is in desperate need. How will we respond?

---

12. I used the term *Islamic fascism* to refer to Islamic movements that, like fascism, aim to recapture a golden age, demand an absolute totalitarian rule, are born of a perceived humiliation, target particular groups as the source of this humiliation, and believe that the new age can only be ushered in by force. Bin Ladin's terrorism movement is an excellent example of this.

2
the poor you will
always have with you

Can we really make poverty disappear?

*Society comprises two classes: those who
have more food than appetite, and those who
have more appetite than food.*

Sébastien-Roch Nicolas de Chamfort

FOR THE PAST twenty years as I have traveled around the world, from Asia to Europe, to Latin America and beyond, I have noticed startling changes occurring in each place that I visit. The most surprising and obvious change has been a decrease in poverty. People's homes, dress, and even the size of their waists clearly reveal that a new era of prosperity is upon us. At times I have wondered if it is my imagination, because the changes I have seen in countries I have visited and revisited have been so dramatic as to defy credibility. In China, I saw a university triple in both campus size and number of students in six months. I saw an island in Thailand that was decimated by the 2006 tsunami rebuild itself in four months. In Krakow, Poland, I visited a shopping mall that looked like it belonged in the middle of America. In the world's most expensive city, Moscow, I frustratingly paid nearly thirty dollars for orange juice, coffee, and cheesecake. On the island of Borneo, I saw housing developments that looked no different from those in suburban Miami. Could all of this really be happening? Even firsthand experience does not make it easy to accept the fact that the world is in surprisingly good shape.

In chapter 1, I suggested that the disappearance of many third-world nations may be key to understanding the twenty-first century. Two-thirds of the world's population is now seeing standards of living improve rapidly. Pockets of the population within these emerging nations are highly plugged into the developed world, and these emerging nations have their fair share of rich people as well. The number of countries disconnected from the global economy is shrinking significantly.[1] Many of the emerging nations may still have millions living in poverty, but they resemble India and China in that they are experiencing rapid upward mobility and are having a significant impact on the global economy. The emerging nations are, in fact, now producing more goods than North America, Europe, and Japan combined.[2]

This does not mean that poverty will go away. Some of the poorest regions of the world, including sub-Saharan Africa and South and Central Asia, still have high birthrates, so the share of the world's poor population is not declining as fast as it could; but birthrates are dropping significantly.

There are also approximately fifty countries that are disconnected from the global economy; these countries are seeing virtually no improvement in living standards. There are far fewer such countries than even fifteen years ago, but the number is still significant. These nations are sometimes referred to as LDCs (least developed countries). Yemen, Haiti, Central African Republic, and Laos are examples of countries in four different regions of the world that will have a very difficult time leaving massive poverty behind. In the future, the rest of the world will need to focus on developing these LDCs and connecting them to the global economy.

Two Hundred Years of Shrinking Poverty

It is true that despite globalization's overall success, we now live in a world where more than twenty thousand people perish each day because of extreme poverty while Bill Gates's $45 billion fortune is enough to pay off the debts of more than twenty of the largest debtor nations in the world. It is statistics like this—which show the dramatic disparity between the richest and poorest—that are used to condemn globalization. But before we start crusading, we need to realize that despite high birth rates among the poor

---

1. By "disconnected from the global economy," I mean that these countries are not integrated economically with the global market to any significant extent, largely due to serious internal weaknesses and failures. They tend to be failed nation-states.

2. For a thorough discussion of this phenomenon, see the September 14, 2006, issue of *The Economist*.

in certain regions of the world, fewer and fewer people are living in extreme poverty.

Prior to the nineteenth century, almost everyone in the world was poor by today's standards—including kings and princes. Stability was never assured; war and total decimation was never far away. The Bible and other ancient texts record the chaotic and threatening conditions in which the ancients lived. Ever wonder why there was so much war and violence in the Bible? Because war and violence in the ancient world was inescapable! Mel Gibson's movie *Apocalypto* provides a good view of the brutal nature of life in much of the world. While the movie takes place roughly five hundred years ago in an era of perpetual warfare and conquest, things were not much different thousands of years before, or hundreds of years later. Until two hundred years ago, there was very little progress overall in raising living standards or increasing personal wealth. Across the centuries of human history, most of the world lived in tight communities and tribes because that was the only way to survive war, disease, and poverty. People could not afford to live as isolated and individualistically as we do now. We no longer live in close communities in our modern world, but it is partly because we live in more peaceful and prosperous societies.

> **Prior to the nineteenth century, almost everyone in the world was poor by today's standards— including kings and princes.**

While the current era of widespread peace began with the conclusion of World War II and the latest round of hyperglobalization commenced with the end of the cold war, the rapid reduction in poverty levels in the West began two hundred years ago with the rise of industrialization, technology, and modern capitalism. This in turn enabled the improvement of living standards in other regions of the world. Since then, every country on the globe has seen a monumental rise in living standards—and as mentioned in chapter 1, that includes Africa. After thousands of years of virtually no fluctuation, the world's per capita income has exploded since 1800; it is nine times greater today. While it is true that the rich are getting richer and the gap between the richest and the poorest is widening, it must be noted that *the poor themselves are also getting richer*. Once again, globalization is not a zero-sum game. Everybody's lot improves substantially over time—but at very different rates. While the quality of life and wealth in East Africa is better than it was in 1800, the quality of life and wealth in the United States has improved phenomenally more in that same time frame. The poorest of America's poor live considerably better than the poor in LDC countries, and they live far more comfortably than the poor (and most of the rich) did in the nineteenth century.

The rising income levels of most of the world's countries in our current era of hyperglobalization have been nothing less than astonishing. The number of poor people in the world in the year 2000 was 650 million, a decline of 800 million since 1980. Since 2000, that number has continued to drop at a faster rate than at any time in history.[3] Even the United Nations, not always known for its optimistic statistics, predicts that global poverty will be dramatically reduced in the coming years, just as it has already been in the past decade. At this rate, the number of those living on less than one dollar a day will drop by 50 percent, down to 16 percent of the total world population, by 2015.[4] This is astonishing.

Furthermore, for the first time since records have been kept, the annual mortality rate for children under the age of five has fallen to less than 10 million—9.7 million in 2006. Latin America is on target to reduce its 1990 child mortality rates by two-thirds by 2015; rates have already dropped 50 percent since 1990. Ethiopia, Malawi, Rwanda, and Tanzania all saw child mortality rates decrease by more than 20 percent in just four years, from 2000 to 2004.[5]

Countries that were never thought of as being wealthy or economically dynamic have transformed themselves into economic juggernauts. China and India have both become vital engines to economic growth throughout the world. They have benefited from the decisions their governments have made to actively participate in globalization. Instead of being written off as poverty-stricken economic basket cases, they are now places where people want to invest and are even (exaggeratedly so) viewed as an economic threat to the West. These two countries, which had the largest populations of poor

---

3. Surjit Bahalla, *Imagine There's No Country: Poverty, Inequality, and Growth in the Era of Globalization* (Peterson Institute, 2002), 139–40, http://bookstore.petersoninstitute.org/book-store/348.html. Bahalla argues that poverty, correctly defined, refers to people living on less than $1.50 per day. His statistics are based on that figure. For a similar definition, see note 4 in chapter 1.

4. *Foreign Policy*, "The List: Five Reasons to Be Thankful This Holiday Season, *Foreign Policy*, November 2007, http://www.foreignpolicy.com/story/cms.php?story_id=4047.

5. Ibid.

people in the world, have transformed themselves in the eyes of the world in a mere ten years. When I first moved to Hong Kong to work in mainland China, Americans assumed China was a place of total poverty. Today, less than ten years later, they think of China as America's primary economic and military superpower rival. While people often overestimate the sophistication of the Chinese and Indian economies, these two nations do have the resources to invest heavily in LDCs, and that is exactly what they are doing. Both countries are also rapidly developing militaries; both have also been increasing the commitment of their military resources in international peacekeeping and humanitarian aid efforts, and will undoubtedly continue to do so as their economic interests abroad increase.

From micro-loans in Bangladesh to startup businesses in China, women are succeeding like never before.

China has spent the bulk of this decade building up its foreign reserves. It now has 1.4 trillion dollars in its piggy bank, and much of that money is being spent on building infrastructure in Africa and Latin America. While rock star Bono and the leaders of the West argue about whether they should give foreign aid packages to Africa, the Chinese are building the roads and the dams that are actually creating new opportunities for wealth generation by Africans themselves. Of course, exploitation occurs, but on an even bigger scale, opportunities are opening up for Africans where none existed before. Countries in Africa were viewed as places for aid and charity, not economic expansion and investment.

We do have to be concerned about the great disparities between the rich and poor within many of these countries, including India and China, but it would be a mistake to assume that *all* of this new wealth only lands in the hands of the wealthy or the emerging middle class. The income of the poor is actually growing at a *faster* rate than the income of the rich. Quality of life continues to improve for even the poorest of the poor. The grand exception to all of this is a large portion of sub-Saharan Africa where population explosion, bad government, poor geography, and diseases like AIDS have caused the quality of life to stay the same or, in some cases, decline. But even in sub-Saharan Africa, there is hope; there has been a slight upturn in recent years.

Today more than ever, many of the world's poor are landowners, which is one of the great keys to upward mobility. Another key to eradicating poverty is the empowerment of women. From micro-loans in Bangladesh to startup businesses in China, women are succeeding like never before. Six of the ten richest self-made women in the world live in China, one of whom is the richest person in the country. Africa is also seeing its fair share of entrepreneurial women. This is important because women are more likely than men to spend the money they earn on items that improve the lives of their children, such as medicine and education. Today, many of the world's poor own televisions, radios, and cell phones. These are not just luxuries; in much of the world, these items provide information, business opportunities, and connectivity.

The majority of the world's poor may not, however, have access to good medical services, education, or capital, and that remains a serious concern and an area where Christians can focus their efforts. It will also be critical to keep an eye on what China and India (and other emerging nations) do in this regard as they invest in the least developed countries.

Reaching Out Across the Rich-Poor Divide

During these past couple of centuries, efforts have been made by missionaries and others to share the wealth with the poorest of the poor. The twentieth century saw a dramatic increase in mission agencies, nonprofit organizations, nongovernmental agencies (NGOs), global relief programs, and foreign aid given by wealthy nations to impoverished nations. The world has been trying to eradicate poverty for a long time.

Globalization has generated so much wealth across the board that a great divide has opened up between the rich and the poor in both developed nations and emerging nations. It is notable that there have not been significant revolutions in most of these emerging nations, particularly China and Russia. While the Chinese government has had to contain over eighty thousand peasant rebellions each year as it tries to address land issues[6], the overall sense in both countries is that life is getting much better, even if some are profiting way more than others. It is important to note that there is much greater goodwill toward globalization in emerging nations than there is in wealthy developed nations. Despite the fact that countries like Canada, Australia, the

---

6. This official figure, widely quoted by China watchers in the West, came from the Ministry on Public Security in the People's Republic of China. In 2005, the number of rebellions surpassed eighty thousand.

United States, and Great Britain are doing very well, there is a much greater sensitivity to the impact of globalization. This may result in poor decisions by these nations to impose barriers to trade and immigration. Globalization may create a divide between rich and poor, but closing off to the world would most likely make the poor poorer in rich nations and poor nations alike. Fortunately, in both developed countries and emerging nations, there is an awareness by the wealthy that they need to give back to society.

One of the most exciting trends of late is the creation of large charity organizations using the wealth of billionaires. Bill Gates may be scandalously rich, but he is giving the vast majority of his wealth away to causes bigger than himself. And frankly, he is outgiving the Christian church. Both Bill Gates and Warren Buffett have committed most of their fortunes to fighting the world's most challenging problems and eradicating poverty. Best of all, the Bill and Melinda Gates Foundation is doing it in a thoughtful way to make sure that the best, most efficient projects are chosen as opposed to just blindly throwing money at various causes. And their generosity is now being mimicked by the nouveaux riche of the emerging world.

> A surprising number of wealthy Asians are Christians as well, and they clearly see the need to give back to society.

The fact that there are so many newly wealthy people in East Asia is a sign of how much has changed. Every single country in East Asia, including economic juggernauts China, South Korea, and Japan, were completely impoverished a mere fifty years ago and were expected to develop more slowly than Africa. Today, with the exception of North Korea, they are all far ahead of where they were after World War II—and that includes the perpetually dysfunctional Philippines.

Many newly wealthy Asians are watching Bill Gates and Warren Buffett carefully. Like the American tycoons of the early twentieth century, these rich Asians realize that they need to invest in their societies or else resentment will reach a boiling point. They are beginning to understand that their countries need them to give to charity. A surprising number of wealthy Asians are Christians as well, and they clearly see the need to give back to society.

In Turkey, billionaire Husnu Ozyegin has spent fifty million dollars of his money building, staffing, and maintaining thirty-six primary schools and girls' dormitories in the poorest parts of the country, making Turkey's richest man the biggest individual supporter of schools other than the government. The world's richest man, Mexican Carlos Slim, has pledged billions for health and education. And Russia's richest man, Roman Abramovich, has invested one billion dollars in the impoverished Arctic area of Chukotka, building schools and hospitals.[7]

With so many things looking up, will the poor always be with us? In Matthew 26:11, Jesus was responding to the indignation of the disciples after a woman had emptied her bottle of expensive perfume in honor of Jesus. Her appreciation of Jesus and her ability to see that he was the Christ affirmed him as he prepared to face his death. His comment about the poor was not a discourse on the nature of global economics and should not be taken out of context. However, because this world is fallen and full of sin, Jesus' words will ultimately be proven right. There will always be poor, because humankind will never be able to attain the level of justice that will be found in the full realization of the kingdom of God. Nevertheless, the latest wave of globalization has already brought nearly a billion people out of dire poverty, and they are headed toward the middle class.

The question for Christians, then, is not whether globalization is good or bad for the poor, but rather how we can bridge the gap between the rich and poor and help the remaining destitute get out of extreme poverty. In other words, how do we utilize this tremendous new era of opportunity in order to care for "the least of these." It is this issue that we will explore in chapter 3.

7. Landon Thomas, Jr., "A New Breed of Millionaire," *New York Times*, December 14, 2007, http://www.nytimes.com/2007/12/14/business/14billionaire.html?ex=1355374800&en=f4254c562 1211edc&ei=5124&partner=permalink&exprod=permalink.

3
searching and planning
for the poor

The poor challenge us to rethink aid strategies.

*It is heartbreaking that global society
has evolved a highly efficient way to get
entertainment to rich adults and children,
while it can't get twelve-cent medicine to
dying poor children.*

William Easterly

OVERALL, GLOBALIZATION CREATES a "borderless" world with more interaction and innovation occurring than would otherwise be the case in a "sealed-off" world. Globalization leads to more opportunities, not only for American businessmen in Dallas, but for fishermen on the Congo River. Most nations will see their poor doing better than they ever have in history. However, the gap between the richest and poorest will increase dramatically in many places. As we have seen, the question is not whether globalization is good or bad for the poor but rather how we can bridge the gap between the rich and poor and help the remaining destitute out of extreme poverty, or what economist Jeffrey Sachs calls "the poverty trap."

Sachs, a well-known macroeconomist, believes that we can easily defeat poverty once and for all. In his intriguing book *The End of Poverty: How We Can Make It Happen in Our Lifetime*, Sachs suggests that the world is wealthy enough to help those people living on less than one dollar a day climb out of poverty. He believes that foreign-aid budgets need to be increased to about $195 billion over the next ten years. If that sounds like an incredible sum of money, consider that in 2006 Americans spent $15 billion on bottled water—think brands like Fiji, Poland Spring, Evian, Dasani, and Aquafina—and that figure is increasing. In ten years, that's $150 billion. Or to take another drink, Americans spent $34.5 billion on coffee in 2005. A more disturbing number is the $120 billion that Americans will spend on pornography over the next ten years—*if* the annual figure remains static at $12 billion per year. More than ever, the money to eradicate poverty is available. The question is whether we are directing it to the right places.

On the other hand, we are all aware that poverty has been with us for a long time, and sometimes it seems that things never get better, no matter how much we spend. Many of us remember the famine in Ethiopia in the 1980s. The world was moved to tears as it watched malnourished children with flies in their eyes waste away in the African desert. In response, the Live Aid concerts raised $80 million to help the impoverished people of Africa. In the end, much of the money and supplies never made it to the starving people. They ended up in the hands of corrupt government officials or were resold on the market. The apparent lack of progress in fighting global poverty, particularly in Africa, has been labeled "Africa fatigue." The world's wealthy countries have gotten tired of giving to massive antipoverty campaigns because there has been little to show for the efforts.

Have Past Programs Made Poverty Worse?

Billions have been spent trying to eradicate third world poverty over these past few decades. For the most part, these efforts have not succeeded. Government corruption, excessively bureaucratic agencies, failure to create institutions that last, poor geography and climate, unstable governments, deeply ingrained cultural habits, and most of all, the limitations of our fallen world and the human structures that we create to deal with the problems are just some of the reasons that antipoverty efforts have failed in the past. Recent literature has suggested that not only do many relief projects fail, but that they actually make the situation worse by ensuring more corruption, more dependence, and more poverty. These are stunning conclusions considering the billions of dollars governments and individuals have spent trying to make the world a better place. Is giving to charity actually making things more difficult for the world's poor?

One of those people who suggest that aid has only made things worse is William Easterly. A professor of economics and senior fellow at the Center for

Global Development, Easterly, who grew up in Africa, worked for the World Bank and has lived in many least developed countries. Having seen many of the problems firsthand, Easterly has written his own book entitled *The White Man's Burden: Why the West's Efforts to Aid the Rest Have Done So Much Ill and So Little Good*. Easterly believes the problem with many relief programs is that they are designed by planners instead of searchers. Planners are those people or organizations that tackle these difficult challenges by making plans from the top down. They believe they have the big solution to the complicated issues, so they create large unwieldy structures or organizations and then they implement them from a distance with little ability to find out whether the goals are met. The World Bank, the International Monetary Fund, the Millennium Project, and countless numbers of NGOs and mission agencies would fall under Easterly's "planners" label.

The apparent lack of progress in fighting global poverty, particularly in Africa, has been labeled "Africa fatigue."

Instead, Easterly would like to see more searchers. Searchers work more organically and have a far keener understanding of the reality on the ground. They look for local solutions and adapt to local conditions. A searcher believes that the reasons for poverty are complex and include political, social, historical, institutional, and technological factors. So for instance, an organization of planners might raise millions of dollars to provide free mosquito nets only to find themselves quite embarrassed when it comes to light that most of the poor who received the nets (which offer protection from deadly diseases) were either used by fishermen to catch fish or were resold on the market. A searcher, on the other hand, would be aware that something like that might take place given the local context, so they might decide to charge five cents per net. The result is that the nets end up in the hands of families that will actually use them for the purpose for which they are intended. The underlying universal principle, in this case, is that people place greater value on something if they have to pay for it rather than getting it for free.

Easterly's approach represents a new wave in thinking about relief projects in general. In 2006, the Nobel Peace Prize went to Muhammad Yunus, a Bangladeshi with a Ph.D. in economics from Vanderbilt University. Distraught over the extreme poverty in his country, Yunus made a list of the poorest forty-two people in a Bangladeshi village. The forty-two poor villagers were captive to their debts. Yunus decided to pay off those debts. The total cost was twenty-seven U.S. dollars. This experience led Yunus to discover that many of the poor were being held down by debts, which were often owed to dangerous people or people charging exorbitant interest rates. Yunus came up with the concept of micro-loans and started Grameen Bank, whose micro-loan program has helped 6.6 million Bangladeshis get out of debt and start businesses.

Today, numerous Christian organizations offer micro-loans. Donors can give as little as five dollars, which will go a remarkably long way in helping someone in a least developed country start a business. The money may go toward buying a sewing machine for a tailor in Afghanistan or a cow for a farmer in Kenya or a phone for a fish merchant in the Congo. The investments are small, but the returns can be large as people get out of poverty and even become successful entrepreneurs. Grameen Bank boasts that 99 percent of its borrowers pay back their loans. Other micro-loan agencies, such as Kiva, an online microlender, also boast of extremely high rates of repayment.

Vampire States and Coconut Republics

There are criticisms of micro-loans. One concern is that the poorest of the poor usually live in areas where mafias or other criminal networks shake down any local businesses or people with money and economic success. Some have argued that many who receive micro-loans are still trapped in a black underground market. The criticism points toward an even more pressing issue: as we continue to analyze relief work, it seems increasingly clear that many factors are needed to help the poor succeed. It is not enough to give individuals money, build hospitals, establish schools, and train people for jobs. There has to be good security and a helpful government as well. In other words, it doesn't do much good to build a new school if a country is so unstable that kids stay home out of fear for their lives. Neither does it do good to build hospitals if no one is trained to staff them and maintain the sensitive equipment. Nor does it work for the poor to finally own a business if they are only going to lose their profits to a local mafia. In other words, many systems must operate efficiently for people to escape the poverty trap; in many places, those systems are not yet in place.

This point is probably understood best by Africans themselves who have endured centuries of Westerners prescribing to them the right kind of medication to take. If you only read one book on helping Africans get out of poverty, go directly to George B. N. Ayittey's magnificent book *Africa Unchained: The Blueprint for Africa's Future*. Security, rule of law, independent media, basic infrastructure—all of these and many more things have been lacking in Africa according to Ayittey. As an African, his voice carries a lot of weight when he argues that for too long, both Westerners and Africans have blamed all of the problems on the West. Furthermore, too many of the solutions have come from the West as well.

For centuries, "vampire states" and "coconut republics" have squandered the talent and potential that lie dormant within while practicing free trade, free markets, and free enterprise. By speaking of coconut

Many of the poor are held down by debts owed to dangerous people.

republics and vampire states, Ayittey refers to countries where nothing functions for anyone except for the elites. This is in contrast to banana republics, which may be corrupt but at least provide some basic services for the people. In coconut republics and vampire states, the people are ignored while corrupt rulers siphon off all the funds meant for the country's development. In some cases, these nations are rich in natural resources, but they only benefit the corrupt leaders. These leaders make their money by acting like vampires, sucking all the wealth out of a country instead of becoming wealthy by their own economic efforts. This kind of corruption can be deeply entrenched, and in our efforts to care for places like Africa, it is very easy to make the wrong choices.

The necessity of considering the whole picture is a tough message for missionaries, NGOs, and other charities to swallow. We have failed to acknowledge that a number of systems and institutions must be functioning well for real change to be lasting and effective. Too often in the past, we have focused on one issue, such as education or water purification or establishing clinics; and to compound the problem, we have done so in isolation from other agencies and the work they are doing. On one hand, a larger effort is needed on the ground to make sure that the necessary systems and institutions are working well as agencies bring aid to poor areas. But on the other hand, we have to make our projects more modest, with higher levels of accountability and more realistic approaches to local problems. It's a tough balance.

Ministry through Business

That, however, is why I am so excited. I believe that one of the greatest untapped resources in the world is the Christian businessman. I recently met a Christian businessman who owns a factory in China. Instead of exploiting his laborers, he has built a factory that has facilities to house the workers' families. No longer does the migrant have to leave family behind in order to provide for them. At this factory, workers are housed, fed, and even hear the gospel. This is a brilliant example of bringing humanity into the capitalist enterprise and raising standards of living while sharing Christ. The realization of this businessman's vision would not have been possible without his faithful heart and the openness that globalization has brought to China.

Living in Hong Kong, I often hear successful Christian businessmen lament that they have "nothing meaningful to contribute to the kingdom of God." I quickly stop them and tell them that in this new era of globalization, they are the people best equipped to bring about economic fairness and to share the gospel. How sad that we have tried to champion the poor by shunning the wealthy and those skilled in business! In an effort to prevent colonialism or to highlight the plight of the needy, we have sometimes gone too far, by ignoring those who are equipped to make a difference in ways that we cannot. Large corporations and the people that run them can be very helpful teammates as we try to tackle these enormous problems.

While the church has often neglected the potential of businessmen, some visionary Christians have taken it upon themselves to network, disciple, and equip businessmen for marketplace ministry. Author Henry Blackaby and businessman Mac McQuiston started the CEO Forum by discipling two businessmen. From those original two, the ministry grew to involve 170 of the top CEOs from Fortune 500 companies. Blackaby has seen CEOs help rebuild Afghanistan, give lectures in economics in China, and bring light and electricity to villages in Kenya. In addition to bringing their faith into the global workplace, these CEOs are able to meet and influence key leaders in non-Christian nations. Blackaby has been asked by business leaders in other nations to set up similar programs in their countries.[1] Alan Ross, founder of Kingdom Companies, believes the global marketplace opens doors to Christianity just as Roman roads once enabled the expansion of Christianity. Kingdom Companies seeks to develop disciples and disciple-makers by making it clear that our spiritual life and work life should not be separate but can be a source of spiritual growth as God uses us to expand his kingdom.[2]

Nathan George created Trade As One to bring products made by the poorest of the poor to consumers in the West. In many cases, the products are made by women who have escaped from sexual slavery or people who are HIV positive.[3] In China, Chinese businessmen are becoming more overt about their faith and the way it can impact their business and society. Stores in China may have biblical names and host Christian gatherings. Nearly thirty executives of large corporations in China are Christians, and their reputation as honest, hard-working, successful, and charitable people is impacting the rest of the business-obsessed nation.[4]

> **How sad that we have tried to champion the poor by shunning the wealthy and those skilled in business!**

There are two things in particular that Christian organizations need right now. The first is the expertise of businessmen. Too many Christian organizations and missionaries are in over their heads trying to tackle the challenges of poverty and development, and that is becoming more and more apparent to many observers. Businessmen can analyze business models and see where we are being inefficient or unrealistic. I also believe that students of missions, missionaries, and seminaries need to be interacting with business schools and vice versa. Imagine business schools offering reduced tuition for NGO workers and missionaries or perhaps missionaries offering business students short-term mission opportunities to learn how their skills can help

---

1. Interview with Henry Blackaby, *Spirit of Revival*, May 2007, http://www.lifeaction.org/soro/godatwork/content/marketplaceministry.htm.

2. www.kingdomcompanies.org

3. www.tradeasone.com

4. Mengai Feng, "Businessmen Bringing New Strength to Spreading Gospel in China," *Christianity Today*, November 12, 2007, http://www.christiantoday.com/article/businessmen.bringing.new.strength.to.spreading.gospel.in.china/14532.htm.

Christian organizations. This can be done and should be done. The complexity of globalization means that being an expert in one subject no longer gets you very far. We need to be learning more and interacting synergistically with people across fields of expertise in order to tackle humanitarian challenges in an effective way.

The second thing that Christian organizations need is long-term investors. The trend among both individual investors and churches is to invest for a short time. People and churches want to see big results quickly. Successful businessmen, on the other hand, understand that an investment may take years to fully mature. They have patience, whereas many Christians in our church planning committees do not. Furthermore, venture capitalists are even willing to lose hundreds of thousands of dollars when they believe in something. American businessmen, in particular, don't believe in failure. They expect to learn no matter what happens and improve the next time. We Christians could use some of that Silicon Valley mentality. The kind of projects that we face in light of the economic disparities globalization creates will require long-term investment and a willingness to stick it out as we seek optimal solutions. Churches supporting mission projects should not jump from project to project and country to country out of boredom. The goal is long-term success, not quick dramatic results that can be played up on the church video screen.

In this new economic world order, there are still injustices, dangers of a new corporate imperialism, and a strong spirit of materialism to contend against. However, we make a grave mistake if we allow the problems to dissuade us. Our analysis of the needs of the poor must be much more nuanced and sophisticated in today's world. As long as this world is governed by human beings, we will always have poverty. But as Christians, we do not want to be part of the problem but part of the solution. Fighting against poverty should not mean rehashing anti-Western tirades, but it does mean that we must intelligently mobilize, give, and make a difference.

the gravitational shift

4

World Christianity is taking the stage.

The urgent ecumenical question is how African, Asian, Latin American, North American and European Christians can live together in the same church, authentically expressing the same faith of Christ and love of Christ.

Andrew Walls

THERE ARE MANY world religions, but there is only one truly global religion—Christianity. While other faiths such as Islam, Baha'i, Sikhism, Jainism, and Hinduism are growing slightly faster than Christianity (due to high birth-rates in southern Asia), Christianity stands alone as the global faith that is growing cross-culturally and through conversion in this era of globalization. You will not find many Guatemalan Hindus in Guatemala. Neither will you find many Korean Muslims in South Korea. Nor is Sikhism or Jainism growing among the mountain tribes of Vietnam or in the large cities of Nigeria. Yet all of these places and many more, from Mongolia to Brazil, are seeing rapid Christian growth because Christianity can go to any geographic location, transform the people, and yet honor the local culture.

This is because Christianity is not tied to ethnic identity, local culture, or geographic location. In Christianity, the relationship between God and humanity is about an intimate personal relationship. The fixed point in Christianity is Jesus Christ, not a mountain range, a particular tribe or caste, or desert city. The result has been that Christianity has truly spread around the globe, permeating societies and cultures that are radically different from one another. Anyone who has ever lived in Brazil or South Korea knows how different the cultures of those two countries are, yet Christianity has exploded in both places and the Christians are completely recognizable to each other. Make no mistake about it: this is a very unusual and beautiful characteristic of Christianity.

One of the great underappreciated beauties of Christianity is that it honors all cultures equally; no one culture can claim to be the closest to God. At the same time, Christianity and the Bible can critique all cultures, pointing out areas where we have fallen short of God's desire for his people. What a stark contrast this is from Islam or Hinduism, which even if they spread out geographically remain so particular to their own region of the world. To become a Muslim or Hindu is to ultimately acquiesce to the Arab or Indian worldview. To become a Christian does not mean becoming Brazilian or South Korean, and certainly not American. The worldview that is formed is Christian: it supersedes culture and yet remains deeply ingrained within the local culture. This is one of the reasons that the argument that Christianity is a Western religion rings hollow.

Is Christianity a Western Religion?

As has been pointed out by numerous scholars, from Kenneth Scott Latourette to Andrew Walls, Christianity, with its unique view of humanity's role in the transmission of the faith, expands, contracts, and sees its center of gravity shift over the centuries. Ever since the Christian message spread from Jerusalem, it has gone out in all directions and transformed cultures and been transformed itself. Christianity is dynamic and does not stay rooted in a particular culture or tradition, unlike Islam, which is still clearly rooted in seventh-century Arab culture, or Esoteric Buddhism, which is so visibly grounded in the culture of Tibet and the neighboring Himalayan countries.

With all the talk about Islamic terrorism and rogue states in the news daily, it's hard to believe that the countries we now call Iraq and Syria were once the strongholds of Christianity. North Africa, too, was a center of Christianity, although today it too is overwhelmingly Muslim. China and India were exposed to Christianity before much of Western Europe, yet we have always thought of those countries as far removed from the center of Christianity.

What is clear is that over the past few centuries, Christianity has come to be perceived as a religion of primarily wealthy, Western people with power. One of the consequences is that the word *missionary* is today viewed pejoratively. For the non-Christian, the word *missionary* conjures up images of Westerners who leave their home countries wearing pith helmets and Bermuda shorts and practice a form of cultural imperialism as they seek to spread the "Western religion" of Christianity. Novels like Barbara Kingsolver's *The Poisonwood Bible* and movies like *At Play in the Fields of the Lord* and *The Mission* capture the sad truth that the Western missionary movement has been careless at times and occasionally destructive.

What is often missed, though, is the incredible amount of good that has been done by the Western missionary movement as it has brought education to countries with none, preserved languages (and cultures)

Defending the Western missionary may increasingly be a thing of the past.

that were dying out, introduced social services in areas where there was once no concern for the poor and helpless, and built hospitals and orphanages, among many other things. But defending the Western missionary may increasingly be a thing of the past. In our new world, it is increasingly obvious that people from non-Western cultures also believe the gospel of Jesus Christ and feel compelled to "go unto all the nations of the world." Christianity did not begin in the West, and it will not end in the West.

The most recent shift has been occurring for some time. In 1900, Africa had approximately ten million Christians, and it was believed that Asia, not Africa, would see the greatest Christian growth in the twentieth century. Instead, it was Africa that embraced Christianity: today, there are just under 400 million Christians in Africa, or slightly less than 50 percent of the population. In other words, there are more Christians in Africa than the total population of the United States and Canada combined.

A Globalizing World Needs a Globalizing Faith

When I recently shared this statistic with a pastor friend of mine, he was incredulous. He simply could not, and would not, believe that Christianity was a major religion in Africa. He was still under the impression that it is a "dark continent" where very few have ever heard of Jesus. "My lifelong dream has been to help take Christianity to Africa," he said. Throughout his life, however, Christianity in Africa has been exploding. Contrary to expectations of the Western church, indigenous African worldviews are often rooted in values shared by Christianity and have proven to be fertile ground for the gospel, producing fruit throughout the continent. Nevertheless, the image of Christianity struggling to penetrate non-Western, and particularly African, societies has persisted.

My pastor friend is not alone. North Americans, in general, have missed the great gravitational shift that is occurring in global Christianity. Our churches have been so focused on spreading the gospel that they have often failed to notice that others have joined us in that effort. North America no longer stands alone as the center of the Christian movement. The country of South Korea, for instance, sends out more missionaries than any other country in the world, excluding the United States. The population of evangelical Christians in Brazil and China will soon outnumber that of North America. In China, the Back to Jerusalem movement hopes to send out one hundred thousand Chinese missionaries into primarily Muslim lands across Asia where Westerners cannot go. Many Christian Filipinos who work as domestic helpers or laborers in the Middle East and East Asia consider themselves missionaries; in fact, many of them belong to organizations that mobilize them precisely for this task. Meanwhile, every day Christians arrive from places like Nigeria to serve as missionaries in North America, in cities such as Phoenix, Houston, and Toronto.

It is easy to believe that North America carries the biggest flag for Christianity. We have the religious history, seminaries, publication houses, television networks, and financial resources to take the gospel to every corner of the world. But even this has been challenged recently: God TV is a worldwide Christian television network broadcasting on satellite and via the Web. Founded in 1998 in London, this company now headquartered in Jerusalem is the fastest-growing Christian broadcaster. And the music of Hillsong Church has put Australia's evangelical movement on the map, and its influence is expanding through international church plants and conferences. This mobilization of people and resources has led to tremendous Christian growth, spiritually and numerically, around the world. But as we enter into this new era, those of us in North America must acknowledge that we have many other brothers and sisters around the world that are also part of the team and that they bring their own knowledge, experience, and resources to the missionary enterprise.

Many Westerners are quick to question the spiritual depth and orthodoxy of the global Christian movement. Nevertheless, the growth of Christianity—particularly evangelical Christianity in Africa, Asia, and Latin America—has been remarkable and has led to many vibrant congregations that are now impacting the world. We must understand that it will take time for some of these new communities to become theologically mature. We must also remind ourselves that Christianity in the West can easily become theologically stagnant and at times heretical. Some are also uncomfortable with the rapid growth of Pentecostalism globally, which is set to have as many people in its fold within the

Evangelical Christianity is decentralized and able to meet needs as they arise.

next twenty-five years as there are Hindus (about one billion). Yes, the Pentecostal emphasis on the supernatural can be abused, but once again, we must not equate Christianity with how Western Christian history has been recorded in Western history books. The spread of Christianity has always been unpredictable.

The reality is that God in his infinite wisdom has chosen to use human beings to work within the church to expand the kingdom of God, and he uses our varied cultures as well, despite their inherent weaknesses. God is the author of cross-cultural exchange. The Bible itself is evidence that we are better when we are sharing with each other across cultures and refining our own cultures. This globalized nature of Christianity means we are constantly brushing up against our own limitations, and both the old centers of Christianity and the emerging centers of Christianity must continually examine themselves and humble themselves before the Lord and each other. It also calls for a great deal of diversity and flexibility. The fact that we now live in a rapidly changing world where people from different cultures are constantly

encountering each other bodes well for the future of Christianity. A globalizing world needs a globalizing faith.[1]

Is the West Finished in its Missionary Role?

Since globalization causes massive change at a rapid speed, it can also cause
displacement and disorientation. Cities erupt overnight before infrastructure
is built to provide for the people. Environmental concerns suddenly become
threatening in regions where they were never an issue. And mass migration
can create entirely new populations of needy people. Because of its loose,
nonhierarchical structure, the evangelical church (and Pentecostal churches
in particular) have the kind of flexibility that allows them to quickly address
the kinds of needs that globalization produces. Much like the Internet and the
World Wide Web, evangelical Christianity is decentralized and able to meet
needs as they arise. This kind of rapid response will be key in the future, and
this is something that we in the West can help with, having been at the forefront of creating this new "flat earth," as Thomas Friedman has called it.[2]

Is there a role on the mission field for Westerners? What is my Western
friend to make of this strange new world where people from Nigeria show
up to work in the church down the street? Is it time for us Westerners to close
up shop? Absolutely not! It simply means that we must become more familiar
with what is happening on the ground in countries around the world. We
do not want to reinvent the wheel and send missionaries or do missionary
projects where competent people are already doing a great job. Instead, we
need to look at each situation closely, analyze the real needs on the ground,
and be prepared to operate from different paradigms. There is still a great
need for Western educators, theologians, health-care workers, pastors, pilots,
and many other professionals to do cross-cultural work. We need churches to
be engaged globally and businesspeople to be brought into the missionary
enterprise. Furthermore, we must continue to be at the forefront of teaching
orthodox Christianity and combating the heresies of our time.

---

1. For a comprehensive discussion of the changing global nature of Christianity, I recommend
Philip Jenkins's books *The Next Christendom* (2002) and *The New Faces of Christianity* (2006), both
published by Oxford University Press.

2. Thomas Friedman, *The World Is Flat: A Brief History of the Twenty-first Century*, 3rd ed (New York:
Picador, 2007).

In some ways, there has never been a greater need or greater opportunity for Western Christians to engage the world. And the world will always need people who will serve others in the name of Jesus Christ. There is clearly something very Christlike about reaching across the cultural divides in the name of *agape*-love. We will always need people to answer the call, leave their homes, and move to distant lands to love the stranger. It is inspiring and it is biblical. But as we do this, we in the West must make sure that as we seek to be a part of the Christian movement around the world, we also see the world as being present within the Christian movement.

5
where have all
the churches gone?

The vanishing act in Europe may be temporary.

Christianity, and nothing else, is the ultimate foundation of liberty, conscience, human rights, and democracy, the benchmarks of Western civilization.

Jürgen Habermas, German intellectual and "methodical atheist," revising his view

PARIS IS MY favorite place in the world to visit. For anyone interested in history, art, or architecture, Paris is not a city but rather a museum come to life. Situated along the River Seine, it serves as the capital of France and of European sophistication. As you walk down the streets of this great world city, Roman, Gothic, Baroque, Rococo, Neo-Classical, Art Nouveau, Art Deco, and modern-day architecture is visible throughout the city—sometimes side by side. No country in the world is visited by more tourists than France (although China will soon surpass it), and no city is more beloved and romanticized. It has been teasingly called "the intellectuals' Disneyland," and the ribbing is probably well-deserved. But despite the occasional pomposity of Parisians and of those who love Paris, it is hard to ignore the fact that this city is deeply rooted in beautiful art, architecture, literature, and philosophy.

The stunning jewels in the Parisian crown are its cathedrals—Notre Dame, Sacre Coeur, and La Sainte Chapelle—all of which leave even nonreligious visitors in awe. The rest of France is also blessed with great cathedrals, from Chartres to Strasbourg. These giant edifices were once the center of village life, provided refuge from barbarian invasions, and often took several generations of masons to complete. They are testaments, not only to the ingenuity of man, but to the beauty of God and the resilience of the Christian church through the medieval era.

Unfortunately, the churches that dot the French landscape are strikingly empty. As in most of Western Europe, Christianity in France is in steep decline, and the rise of secularism there is an example of the wider trend that is occurring across the Christianized West. From Canada to Spain, non-immigrant populations have largely abandoned Christianity and often religion altogether.

While Christianity is flourishing in areas we once viewed as extremely resistant to the faith, the "heartland of Christianity" has become a bastion of secularism. In Italy, the home of the pope, fewer and fewer Italians follow the instructions of the Roman Catholic Church, including those regarding the controversial issue of birth control. Italians, always associated with large families, now have the lowest birthrate in Europe. Germany, the birthplace of the Protestant Reformation, ranks near the bottom in church attendance, while Britain sees a church close and a mosque open every week. Ireland, a country whose name was synonymous with religious violence for much of the last century, is now a country whose citizens are so apathetic about Christianity that priests have to be imported from Africa to hold mass. And Poland, which saw Catholicism and the Polish workers' movement Solidarity begin the process that brought down the Iron Curtain, is now a country of spiritually apathetic Catholics.

> The "heartland of Christianity" has become a bastion of secularism.

This secularization has created what I call *ironic mission fields:* Places such as Germany, Italy, and Switzerland where Christianity was not only widely accepted but even central to the history of the faith are now in desperate need of missionaries and the good news they bring. It may not seem as romantic or as exotic as supporting missionaries in Africa or China, but ministries in Europe are in serious need of support. The spiritual environment of European ministry is just as difficult, if not more difficult, as many of the areas that generate the most interest among supporters.

It is not just that Europeans are rejecting Christianity; increasingly, they are not even sure what it is. Whether it is the facts surrounding the life of Jesus or the major Christian holidays, Europeans are not likely to know much about the Christian faith. Telling the average European that you are an evangelical Christian is about the same as telling them that you are an alien space ranger from the planet Loony, though you are likely to get more respect if you say the latter.

Europe's Distrust of Religion

Europeans are, however, well-versed in European history, which is replete with violence and corruption, much of it emanating from the Christian church. Not only was Europe the birthplace of Christendom (i.e., the Holy Roman Empire, in which European political states were under the authority of the church), but it was also where the Christian church ultimately, and with great hostility, divided into three branches: Orthodox, Roman Catholic, and Protestant. It was in Europe that Christianity got organized, institutionalized, and then deeply divided. Those divisions resulted in wars—not small wars, but wars that resulted in centuries of violence and millions killed. In Europe, religion is often perceived as dangerous in a way that it is not in the United States, where the separation of church and state protected the reputation of the church in the eyes of the people.

While Europe was the birthplace of the first truly global Christian institution (the Holy Roman Empire and the Roman Catholic Church) to amass global power and wealth under the banner of Christendom, it was also the birthplace of the Enlightenment, in which reason challenged the authority of God and the church. While secularism did not lead Europe into a new era of peace (after all, World War I and World War II devastated the continent), it did ultimately result in the end of respect for the authority of the church. In most of Europe today, the State has much more credibility than the church in the eyes of the people, and it is the State that has held European society together in the wake of Christendom's demise, not the church.

The trauma of two world wars and the nationalistic racial hatred propagated by the Nazi regime has also made Europe skittish about any religious group claiming absolutes. Christianity has been marginalized for the most part, and Islam has been appeased out of fear. Once again, Europeans are far more conscious of history: they remember the Muslim invasions and Christian empires of the past.

Neither has it helped that many churches in Europe are state-supported and do not need to compete in the religious marketplace. Buildings are funded, clergy salaries are paid, and even "missionaries" are sent out. The result is a calcified church that just exists as an institution rather than as a living, breathing community of faith looking to transform the world.

Signs of Hope?

The death of Christianity in Europe as represented by organized religion does initially seem disheartening. But we should not mistake Europe's dismissal of institutional Christianity as a rejection of all things spiritual. It is true that there are few places where Christianity or any kind of spirituality generates the excitement found at a European football match (a substitute for transcendent community perhaps?), but Europeans are still seeking spirituality in various ways: some healthy and some unhealthy. Europe now has its fair share of adherents to traditional witchcraft and crop worship. Numerous cults, including alien cults, have also sprung up. And many Orthodox and Roman Catholic believers continue to practice their faiths with great devotion and faith, even if they ignore the clergy and the institutional church. With Eastern Europe now open to visitors, many Europeans are flocking to pilgrimage sites that were once difficult to reach, such as the shrine to Mary in Czestochowa, Poland, which houses a painting that is reputed to have been painted by Saint Luke. In fact, in this new age of globalization, pilgrimages are so popular that a low-cost carrier has started up specializing in flights to Catholic pilgrimage sites, such as Lourdes, Fatima, and Czestochowa. Another sign of hope is the renewal movement occurring among both Catholic and Protestant youth. On a recent trip to Germany, I witnessed young people from all over Europe flocking to hear the Pope.

The Faith of Immigrants

In many places throughout Europe, the greatest religious fervor is found in the immigrant communities of people from the emerging world and least developed countries. France, for instance, is home to an enormous population of Muslim immigrants, mainly North Africans, leading to major confrontations between Islamic religious culture and French secularism. As the Muslim population has risen, tensions have soared between the deeply religious immigrants and the very secular French. These tensions have been compounded by a lack of integration into French culture and high unemployment among immigrant youth. And in Britain, it is Islam, not Christianity, that is about to become the nation's primary religion.

Fortunately, Paris, London, and many other European cities also have very dynamic Christian immigrant churches. The largest Christian church in Europe is located in the Ukrainian city of Kiev and is pastored by an African. London is now home to several megachurches, and there is a renewed interest in Christianity among English youth. In the suburbs of Paris, Caribbean and West African evangelical churches are drawing in people attracted by the vibrant, multicultural worship. Even in the highly secular countries of Scandinavia, some congregations are seeing surprising growth. In major cities across Europe, such as Rome and Munich, it is not unusual to find Christians from Wuhan, China, sharing the gospel near the major tourist sites. The image of the West being re-Christianized by people from the "non-Christian, third world" is not only ironic for those of us with the old images of the past in our head but also deeply emblematic of the global nature of Christianity.

> **Europe's dismissal of institutional Christianity is not a rejection of all things spiritual.**

While it is true that the most active Christian growth is occurring in immigrant communities in Europe, it is certainly possible that these immigrant churches will be influential in bringing Christ to the native populations of Europe. Nearly every Western European country is reducing social services, as well as funding for the state-supported church. Globalization is forcing European nations to become more competitive. They are getting wealthier, but they are also restructuring their economies and societies. This may well be a perfect time for evangelical Christianity to engage in Europe, considering Christianity's sensitivity to local needs and its tremendous flexibility to start meeting the needs of the average European in ways not previously imagined. The death of the institutional state church in Europe could easily lead to the birth of vibrant, *agape*-filled communities serving in Christ's name.

Although evangelical Christianity is often viewed in Europe as outside of mainstream Christianity and even cultlike, doors are opening across Europe.

While Europeans do need a better understanding of evangelical Christianity, we evangelicals from North America must also be patient with Europeans and seek to understand how their history, which is also a vital part of our own Christian history, has led them to their current state of belief.

Underneath the secular veneer, many Europeans hold core values that echo Christian values. A concern for human rights and a belief in the importance of every human being, environmental activism, a willingness to share their wealth with society's less fortunate, a commitment to foreign aid, and strong demands for peace as opposed to war in dealing with global affairs— these are all signs that the imprint of Christianity remains on the European heart. We can critique the European welfare state, disagree with its foreign policy, and reject Europe's liberalism, but we must look more closely to see that many of these tendencies are actually rooted in timeless truths deposited by Christianity over the centuries.[1] Europe's secularism is the result of human failure in representing and interpreting the message of Christ; it is not the failure of Christ himself.

---

1. Scholars who have argued that Western secular humanism and contemporary European secularism are rooted in Christianity include sociologist Philip Jenkins, historian Lamin Sanneh, sociologist Rodney Stark, and historian Thomas E. Woods.

6
students are plentiful,
but teachers are few

Education is a key to transforming the world.

*To educate a person in mind and not in morals
is to educate a menace to society.*

Theodore Roosevelt

YOU HAVE HEARD of Harvard, Cambridge, and Stanford, but have you heard of Allam Iqbal Open University, Indira Gandhi National Open University, or Sukhothai Thammathirat Open University? These last three schools (in Pakistan, India, and Thailand respectively) are part of the latest trend in global higher education: the mega-university. In this new age of rapid technological change, more and more people in the developed nations, emerging nations, and least developed countries are seeking postsecondary degrees. From South Africa to Iran, new mega-universities are being launched that are able to handle more than one hundred thousand students by taking advantage of the Internet. Increasingly, evangelical universities are also playing a large part in meeting the demand for education, which may provide the Christian movement with new opportunities for outreach. The emphasis on education is vital, because education is the single most important factor in determining whether people will be relegated to a life of absolute poverty or not. Globalization creates more pressure on everyone to be able to read, write, and speak well. In developed nations, as well as emerging nations and least developed countries, everyone will need to invest far more in education in the future.

Mega-universities have traditionally been state-supported schools, but increasingly, rich and poor countries alike are unable to sufficiently fund higher education. (I recently read of a university in India that has not had money to publish a course catalogue since 1973.) Countries that were once closed to privatization, such as Kenya and Uganda, are increasingly loosening their grip and establishing new rules for chartering universities because they do not want to be limited by the choices facing their best and brightest people: go overseas for college education or remain at home without a college education due to the lack of space in state universities.

Christian Institutions Reach Out

Throughout the world, students increasingly want to receive a good education in English under a Western-style educational system. For better or for worse, English has become the language of global scholarship as well as the language of information technology and the Internet. Sadly, in many cases, the new private universities are failing to provide quality educations to their enthusiastic students. One bright spot however, is the work of evangelical universities, which are not only equipping students to compete in our new technological age but are also addressing local needs, such as agriculture and biotechnology, while remaining true to their Christian foundations. Sung Kyul University in South Korea and Central University College in Ghana are two examples of schools that are doing an excellent job of offering a Christ-centered education that equips students for the modern world.

There are challenges of course. Some of the countries that most need help on the educational front are currently closed to Christianity. Others still impose significant bureaucratic hurdles. In many places, lower-income youth are still having difficulty finding a place to study. However, one cannot help but feel that a new door of opportunity is opening up around the world.

Also new to the educational landscape are organizations and foundations that provide specialized educational services in emerging nations. In many countries, the need is not limited to simply a high-level education enabling the student to compete on the global stage; ethical training is needed as well. Many countries embracing free-market economics suffered for years under totalitarian rule, poorly planned centralized economies, corruption, and institutional and social breakdown; these societies are often marked by a general distrust, not only between the people and the government, but between individuals as well. These "low-trust societies," as Francis Fukuyama has called them, are countries that desperately need to produce a new generation of students who will go into business and government and bring ethics to economics, create a strong rule of law in the legal systems, and inspire confidence in public and private institutions. These newly emerging nations need a spiritual makeover as well as an economic and educational makeover. This provides tremendous opportunities for Christian educators.

For instance, after the collapse of the Soviet Union, the former Soviet Republic of Kazakhstan found itself needing to adjust its economy as it opened up to the world after years of suffering under a corrupt, inefficient planned economy. In some fields, the Soviet system of higher education excelled, such as in the hard sciences, but in other areas, it was woefully unprepared for the challenges of this new world order. East Kazakhstan State University was one of many colleges feeling the pressure to adequately prepare its students to compete globally. There was a great need to learn English and

English has become the language of global scholarship as well as the language of the Internet.

to receive a top-quality education that would introduce free-market economics to the students. Western expertise was greatly needed, not just for the future of the school, but for the whole country.

In 1997, Marshall Christensen, former president of Warner Pacific College—a Christian college in Portland, Oregon—founded the Marshall Christensen Foundation for International Higher Education, which established a visiting faculty program for American teachers to take their business expertise to East Kazakhstan State University. Not only were students exposed to teachers of exceptional quality, but top students were also given the opportunity to do business internships in the United States and to live with host families. The foundation also offers scholarships to students who want to pursue MBAs at Christian colleges in the United States before returning to Kazakhstan. Today the university, which has about three thousand students, is known as Kazakh-American Free University.

As students at the university were training in business, it became very clear to them that transparency and accountability in business are key components to success and that these require more than just adjustments to business models: they require a radical change in individual hearts and in society at large. The business training accentuated the need for more ethical teaching. The International Servant Leadership Program was established, offering exceptional third-year students focused leadership training and mentoring. Ultimately, the moral character of students is reshaped as they focus on leadership qualities such as personal integrity, core values, and relationships.

Liberal Protestants have, at times, displayed a tendency to demonize capitalist business people as exploitive and superficial, arguing that they are detached from real people and real social problems. The antiglobalization movement has often relied on this kind of caricature to fuel its campaign. Conservative evangelicals, on the other hand, have sometimes downplayed the importance of education, particularly when it is not overtly Christian. The anti-intellectual tendency of evangelicalism has been harmful to the Christian faith, and it is increasingly harmful in a world being transformed by globalization. We need to move beyond that. As the Marshall Christensen Foundation, Sung Kyul, and other institutions show us, this new world offers opportunities for Christian education and outreach, and we will need teachers from many diverse fields teaching in a variety of settings. The students are plentiful, but the teachers are few.

good morning, vietnam!

This battle-scarred nation is a hotbed of growth.

Everyone here is ready to go to prison for their faith.

A Vietnamese Christian

EMERGING NATIONS BRAZIL, China, Vietnam, and Nigeria are just four examples of countries whose economies are growing as they never have before. Each is trying to transform itself from a nation of poverty and poor productivity into a major economic force on the global stage. The openness to new ideas and the massive changes and shifts that occur during such times of transition offer great opportunities for Christianity to flourish. In unexpected places throughout the world, God is raising up his church. Whether it's Nigerian believers immigrating to Europe or taking their Christianity to North America, Brazilian Pentecostals setting up churches and social services in the poorest neighborhoods in Rio de Janeiro, or Christians in China contributing to the building of a civil society from scratch, globalization's economic and cultural transformations open the door for spiritual transformation as well. Globalization and modernization tend to make people more religious, not less religious.

I recently returned from a trip to Vietnam, where I had the privilege of meeting with some leaders who represent the future of Christianity in this beautiful yet scarred Southeast Asian country. The leadership and missionary efforts of these new Christians will shake the world and transform our views of the Christian faith. At the end of the Vietnam War, the Americans fighting there could scarcely have imagined that this country would one day not only boast a vibrant economy but would also be a source of Christian growth.

Despite its small physical footprint (it's only thirty miles wide in some places), Vietnam has a population of eighty-two million people—roughly one-fourth the population of the United States. This communist country has undergone massive change over the past few decades. But for many Americans, our images of Vietnam continue to be defined by the conflict of the 1960s and '70s. The Vietnam War left its imprint on both nations and epitomized the messy and destructive low-intensity conflicts that broke out around the world during the cold war.

After the Vietnam War, communism led the nation into dire poverty. Attempts to open up the economy began in the mid-1990s only to be severely curtailed by the government. What seemed like a turning of the tide soon became a major disappointment for Japanese, European, and American businessmen hoping to see Vietnamese entrepreneurialism unleashed. Foreign investment declined significantly.

Today, however, the clouds are truly breaking. Vietnam is now a member of the World Trade Organization and is attempting to liberalize its economy. The economy is currently growing at a rate of 8.4 percent annually—second worldwide only to China. The number of people living on less than a dollar a day has decreased from 51 percent to 8 percent since 1990, and the number of foreign visitors has increased a staggering 20 percent per year.[1] The country is transforming rapidly into a peaceful and economically successful nation. The famous Ho Chi Minh Trail road system, which passes along the Truong Son Range and facilitated the movement of soldiers and war supplies from North Vietnam to battlefields in South Vietnam, is now lined with golf courses for tourists who want to take a more leisurely trek through the jungle.

Vietnamese Christians represent the new face of Christianity in emerging nations.

Vietnam is running about fifteen years behind China in its development. However, if it remains open, I believe it will close the gap quickly. The intelligence, work ethic, and adaptation skills of the Vietnamese people are so great that I believe the Vietnamese will surpass the Chinese in the speed of

1. Keith Bradsher, "Vietnam's Roaring Economy Is Set for World Stage," *New York Times*, October 25, 2006, http://www.nytimes.com/2006/10/25/business/worldbusiness/25vietnam.html?ex=1319428800&en=d30d15747694acae&ei=5088&partner=rssnyt&emc=rss.

their integration into the global economy. In many ways, the Vietnamese seem to exhibit a much greater aptitude for dealing with foreigners and for understanding Western business ways than do the Chinese; perhaps it is the influence of French colonialism.

Vietnam is arriving on the global stage, and just in time. Over 60 percent of the Vietnamese were born after the Vietnam War ended in 1975, which means that the country has one of the world's youngest populations. Riding on a scooter through the city of Ho Chi Minh, I saw few people who appeared to be older than thirty. These young people have no memories of the war and have high expectations for the future. I could not have been more impressed by the young people I met throughout the country, and fortunately, many are interested in Christianity.

Persecution of Vietnamese Christians

Roman Catholicism, Buddhism, and the indigenous religion of Cao Dai, which worships an odd mixture of deities that includes Buddha, Confucius, Jesus, and French Novelist Victor Hugo, are influential in Vietnam, but the government has been quite hostile toward evangelical Christianity, particularly in areas inhabited by ethnic minorities.

In the mountains and on the border with Laos and China, Christians are still persecuted and killed. Access to these Christians remains limited. Persecution can involve anything from the burning of churches and confiscation of materials to torture and rape. Churches must be registered and limit their activities to work within the church. In the major cities, Christianity seems to be able to function with less interference from the government, although proselytizing outside of the church is strictly forbidden. As is the case with China, the Vietnamese government fears the demise of centralized control at the hands of decentralized religious groups. And as in China, this has led to a lot of underground Christian ministry. Persecution has only added fuel to the fire. The result has been some truly magnificent growth in Christianity—particularly among minority groups in the mountains. In Lao Cai Province, there were no Christians in 1991. After seven years of underground missionary effort, there were seventy thousand believers. You do the math.

The amount of change that will occur in the next ten years will open the door even further to Christianity. But it will also bring great temptations for the young church. Already, there is the danger that Christians from other countries will recklessly give too much money to the young church and foster division, competitiveness, and denominationalism. But the Vietnamese have proven themselves to be hard workers, fast learners, and prepared for anything that comes their way.

Vietnamese Christians represent the new face of Christianity in emerging nations. It is nonwhite, mission-minded, and overwhelmingly open to the supernatural. This spiritual openness is coupled with a motivation and resilience that is lacking in many churches in the West. The Vietnamese have shown the world time and time again that they do not quit amid persecution and war—even if the persecution comes from their own people and the war from Satan himself.

At the same time, the young Christians in these newly emerging nations like Vietnam need wise teaching in regard to structuring their churches and missionary efforts for long-term success. An influx of money, a competitive spirit, and a lack of solid theological training have the potential to create divided communities that could burn out before they burn bright. Ignoring the new face of Christianity is not the answer, but neither is romanticizing it. All cultures and all people suffer the effects of sin.

I recently spoke to an American businessman involved in a foreign venture in Vietnam. He shared with me that all of the foreign business managers he works with love employing the Vietnamese because of their work ethic and adaptability. I told him I felt the same way about working with the Christian church in Vietnam. They are delightful, beautiful people with great smiles and hearts to match. While the global business community profits from the unique gifts of the Vietnamese people, perhaps we in the West will profit from a prophetic Vietnamese church.

part II
the challenges

8
scourge of the
new century

Sexual slavery is in our own backyard.

*So enormous, so dreadful, so irremediable did
the trade's wickedness appear that my own
mind was completely made up for Abolition.*

William Wilberforce

IN THE AFRICAN country of Ghana, numerous forts dating back to the seventeenth century hug the coastline. These ancient structures, with names like Cape Coast Castle and Elmina, were known as "factories"; they are a testament to one of the darkest institutions in history—the trans-Atlantic slave trade. Inside the castles, filthy dungeons held captured slaves before they were shipped as cargo to Europe and the New World. A great number of the slaves died in these dungeons or during the trans-Atlantic voyage. Those that survived endured physical suffering and humiliation at the hands of their masters. If it were not for the efforts of the British anti-slavery movement, which included evangelicals such as William Wilberforce, Thomas Clarkson, and Granville Sharp, slavery might have continued for decades longer than it did—having been abolished in Britain under the Slave Trade Act of 1807. Today, visitors to the castles of Ghana often find themselves emotionally overwhelmed as they enter the halls where thousands of slaves started their long journey of suffering and exploitation.

We look back at that era in horror and wonder how it could have taken so long for people—particularly Christian people—to mobilize and fight such an inhumane institution. We assume that places like Cape Coast and Elmina could not exist in today's world. But we are mistaken. Today's slavery castles are not off the coast of Africa, but in our own backyard. Today's "castles" have names like La Guardia, Heathrow, LAX, and Schiphol. Every year, millions of slaves pass through our modern, high-tech, security-obsessed airports on a long journey of suffering and sexual exploitation. The growth of the transnational sex trade of women and children may be one of the greatest struggles against evil that we have ever faced. The slaves are scattered across the globe, as far away as Sri Lanka and as close as suburban New Jersey, yet most Christians remain oblivious to the tragedy in their midst.

Sexual slavery is not new. During the Arab slave trade in the ninth century, women were used as slaves for sex. More recently, during World War II, women throughout East Asia were used by Japanese soldiers as "comfort women"—an issue that is still highly sensitive throughout the region. The Old Testament prophet Elijah railed against the Baal worship and the temples filled with sex slaves. But today's sexual slavery is truly a transnational global enterprise. Organized crime syndicates take advantage of cell phones, lax immigration laws, and ease of travel and communication to do their business. The Russian mafia in Israel, for instance, regularly captures women from places like Albania, Lithuania, and Romania. The captured women may then be transported by trucks and planes to Mexico before being smuggled across the American border or worked in brothels in Mexico.

The Methods of Enslavement

As unbelievable as it might sound, more people are caught up in human trafficking (slave trade) today than in the African slave trade of centuries past. Approximately 800,000 people are trafficked across international borders annually. This does not include those being held captive within their own countries. In this new form of slavery, 80 percent are women and children, and 50 percent are under the age of eighteen.[1] While we tend to think of the drug trade and the illegal arms trade as being the cash cows for criminals, sexual slavery, which already generates thirty-one billion dollars in profits annually, is the wave of the future. When you consider that an African boy or girl can easily be purchased for twenty U.S. dollars, the numbers become truly sickening.

---

1. U.S. Department of State, *Victims of Trafficking and Violence Protection Act of 2000: Trafficking in Persons Report 2007* (Washington, DC: U.S. Department of State, 2007), http://www.state.gov/g/tip/rls/tiprpt/2007/.

Nearly all of the women are tricked into forced prostitution. Women from poor countries are promised jobs as waitresses, dancers, or cleaners. Sometimes they are brought to a country by a "boyfriend" who happens to work for a criminal organization. By the time the woman finds out that her romance was a setup and her romantic suitor a member of a criminal organization, it is too late: she may be in a foreign country, locked inside a guarded hotel room, and forced to perform sex acts. The problem has grown so widespread that in some countries (e.g., Eastern Europe), young women have started to become suspicious of men offering them jobs. In response, the organized criminals have simply shifted tactics and started using women to recruit women. Others are tricked by "marriage organizations" that convince women that they are being matched with prospective husbands when in reality a trap is being set for them.

Globalization allows the evil to be decentralized.

Even more tragic are the many cases of women sold into slavery by their own families. Then there are the horrific stories of children purchased from orphanages in places like Moldova, Sri Lanka, and Romania.

Once the women are captured, they are beaten and sexually abused in order to make them compliant. If need be, captors will torture or kill a woman in front of the other captured women in order to show that they are in total control. These modern-day slavers make a point of knowing where a woman's family lives so that they can threaten to kill or capture them if the woman does not perform. A simple peasant woman suddenly in a foreign country thousands of miles away from home may submit to her "owners" instead of rebelling simply out of fear and disorientation. Even if a woman escapes and goes to the authorities, there are far too many middlemen, spread out across too many continents, for the slavery network to be taken down. The organizational means enabled by globalization allow the evil to be decentralized.

Locked in a motel or house in places like London or New York, these women may be forced to work in twenty-four hour shifts servicing between forty and eighty men a day. Deborah Finding of the Poppy Project in Great Britain, which works with victims of the trade, was shocked to discover that on Christmas day one woman in London had to have sex with eighty-eight men. "I thought maybe there were eighty-eight men in the whole of London who are going to pay someone for sex on Christmas Day. But that's one woman, one brothel in one bit of Soho, and to me that just shows you the scale of the problem," she told PBS's *Frontline*.[2]

I was shocked to discover that one of my favorite areas of London is ridden with brothels keeping women hostage—right under everyone's nose but completely out of view. Behind the facades of the beautiful buildings in downtown London, women are being held against their will, unable to see the light of day. In these places, one woman alone can generate as much as $250,000 per year for the crime network.[3] The women themselves get paid nothing. In fact, they are often charged for their transportation and start out their "careers" as slaves tens of thousands of dollars in debt. At any time, they may be fined by their owners thousands of dollars. The idea that the women will ever make a penny is ludicrous. They are slaves in every sense of the word.

If by chance, the women, girls, or boys are able to escape and return home, it is usually pointless. In almost every culture around the world, these people are considered damaged goods—unworthy of marriage and disgraceful to their families. This is especially the case in Asia, which is a global producer of exploited children and women. In Asia, a woman's value as a human being (which is not high to begin with in most Asian cultures) plummets to nothing once her virginity is lost. Furthermore, even in the West, many people confuse the issue of sex slavery with prostitution, assuming that these women have chosen to go overseas to sell their bodies when, in fact, they are innocent victims being trafficked on the market as commodities.

A Global Problem Needs Global Mobilization

Less than nine years after the end of the cold war, approximately fifty thousand slaves were entering into the United States each year, many of them from the former Soviet Union.[4] Over the course of a decade, the number adds

---

2. Interview online with Deborah Finding by PBS *Frontline*, http://www.pbs.org/wgbh/pages/frontline/slaves/needs/finding.html.

3. Interview online with Victor Malarek by PBS *Frontline*, http://www.pbs.org/wgbh/pages/frontline/slaves/needs/malarek.html.

4. Janice G. Raymond and Donna M. Hughes, *Sex Trafficking of Women in the United States: International and Domestic Trends* (Coalition Against Trafficking in Women), March 2001, http://www.uri.edu/artsci/wms/hughes/sex_traff_us.pdf.

up to the size of a fairly large American city. But the United States is not the worst country in regard to its tolerance for sexual slavery. According to the 2007 U.S. State Department Report on Human Trafficking, Sudan, Sierra Leone, Venezuela, Ecuador, and Bangladesh are among the worst offenders. Also on the watch list as countries deeply entangled in the sex slave trade are Japan, Mexico, Thailand, Turkey, Russia, Greece, Guatemala, Qatar, and many others.[5] Every continent, except Antarctica, is heavily represented on the watch list as far as involvement in human sexual slavery is concerned. It is a scathing indictment of human society that, regardless of our various religions, cultures, and social mores, our nations engage in slavery because there is so great a demand for it. Sexual abuse is a global epidemic empowered by the new technologies and interconnections of our globalized world.

Most of the world's sex slaves come from population segments left behind in the new global order.

Despite the fact that globalization will rapidly raise living standards across the world, it does creates a huge gap between rich and poor. Most of the world's sex slaves come from population segments that are being left behind in the new global order. Tackling the current sex slave trade will be just as difficult, if not more so, than Wilberforce's crusade against the slavery of his day. It will require a war on corruption in source countries, higher standards of accountability from all governments in regard to illegal immigration, and numerous programs to help train, educate, and integrate or repatriate sex slaves. Most of all, it will take enormous amounts of activism on the part of global citizens. This is the kind of issue that will demand marches on Washington, large-scale petitions, and answers from politicians. And once again, it will most emphatically need the hands of Christians working together for the freedom of the innocent.

There are numerous secular organizations joining the fight against human sex trafficking, including anti-slavery.org, Coalition to Abolish Slavery and Trafficking, Global Alliance Against Trafficking Women, UNICEF, Human Rights Watch, Global Fund for Women, and many others. Fortunately, there are already numerous Christian organizations working to end this trade and to meet the needs of its victims, organizations like Christian Aid, Tear Fund,

5. U.S. Department of State, *Trafficking in Persons Report 2007.*

and World Vision. Even more promising are the number of Christian business-men who are opening up businesses that employ former prostitutes and sex slaves, giving them the chance to learn skills for a good wage in a safe environment. In Cambodia, which has been a hotbed for sexual slavery as well as a popular destination for pedophiles, Hagar Catering, in Phnom Penh, not only trains and employs women recovered from the sex slave industry but works to prevent their exploitation by investing in their schooling, feeding them, providing parenting groups, and offering spiritual guidance.

Many are fighting this scourge, but we need many others to join the fight. The question for Christians now at the dawn of this new century is whether we will sleep as the castles of the slave trade are built on our very own shores.

9
the threat
is different now

Transnational terrorism is more dangerous.

*We are fighting an enemy who has no
strategic purpose in anything he does, whose
actions have significance only in terms of his
own fantasy ideology.*

Lee Harris

THE ACT OF war came completely by surprise. It was a battle fought not with an army, but rather an unexpected asymmetrical attack by terrorists. The once mighty nation suddenly seemed vulnerable, its powerful military unable to predict and stop the attack. These enemies were not soldiers in any nation's army, but rather they were acting independently and were not tied to any one geographical location. There were no real leaders or generals; instead, there were many leaders in many different places. The enemy operated in small cells, which cut down on the need for communication. Once these small, highly mobile units attacked, they could easily disappear and find safe harbor. Warfare would never be the same.

A description of al Qaeda's surprise attack on the United States on September 11, 2001? No, this is what Alexander the Great came up against when he unexpectedly encountered the Scythians more than three hundred years before the birth of Christ. The unexpected methods of attack and the terror that they caused made a seemingly invincible military stop in its tracks, forcing Alexander to reevaluate his methods. Today, the battle between Alexander and the Scythians plays out on a larger, more lethal scale, and it will continue to shape the new world order for decades to come.

Terrorism and the use of asymmetrical attacks to achieve political and religious gain have been around for a long time. Centuries after Alexander's encounter with the Scythians, Hassan i Sabbah and the Hashshashin (from which we get the word *assassin*) sought to terrorize and destroy the leadership of the eleventh-century Islamic Abbasid Caliphate and introduce their own Islamic doctrine. And in England in 1605, Catholic terrorists attempted to destroy the English Parliament and kill Protestant King James I. Alexander the II in Russia was assassinated by members of the People's Will, whose political goals included abolishing Russian autocracy.

In recent decades, Britain and Spain have both had to deal with terrorism, from the IRA and ETA respectively. In Southern Asia, Hindu suicide bombers have wrecked havoc, successfully assassinating Rajiv Gandhi in 1991 and blowing out the right eye of Sri Lankan president Chandrika Kumaratunga in 1999. Tokyo, perhaps the safest large city in the world, suffered a terrorist attack on its subways in 1995 when the Aum Shinrikyo cult (now known as Aleph) released sarin gas in the subways. Even in the United States, terrorism reared its ugly head long ago with the Ku Klux Klan organization, which at its peak in the 1920s had a membership of six million and sought to intimidate and kill African Americans.

We have encountered terrorism before, and in every case, the terrorist groups disappeared in time or were neutralized. Terrorists have rarely achieved their goals in the long run. If that is the case, what makes this current "war on terror" different from the struggles against barbarity in other eras?

5 Reasons Why Terrorism Is Different Today

The decentralized nature of modern-day terrorism, which leads to rogue, unaccountable, independent cells, combined with a pursuit of incredibly lethal technology and a desire to destroy for the sake of destruction (as opposed to fighting for a particular attainable objective) makes today's terrorism one of the world's greatest problems. The military campaigns in Iraq and Afghanistan have led many to believe that the terrorist threat has been exaggerated. In time, however, the decentralized, technologically sophisticated, and nihilistic nature of the world's most dangerous terrorist organizations will put the issue back in the headlines. The convergence of these characteristics threatens global stability on a scale never seen before.

First, today's terrorism is larger in scope and has far larger goals than in previous eras. Throughout history, the goals of terrorists have been fairly limited. Terrorism involved the assassinations of kings and princes, the defeat of an army in one fixed location, or the terrorizing of particular populations for limited goals. Even as late as September 10, 2001, the terrorist organizations we worried about had very limited goals. Hijackers in the 1980s usually demanded the release of prisoners from Israeli jails or statehood for Palestine. Terrorists in Ireland, Sri Lanka, and Spain were attempting to carve out a piece of land from an existing nation-state. Great wars and great campaigns were the stuff of large empires and nations doing battle, not small, decentralized groups. Prior to our current era, technology had not enabled a small group of actors to have such global aspirations.

> The convergence of these characteristics threatens global stability on a scale never seen before.

This is no longer the case. Today, the changes brought by globalization allow terrorism to be truly transnational. Open borders, cheap and powerful methods of communication, well-educated terrorists, technological innovation, and international financial networks have made terrorism far more expansive. While groups like the Tamil Tigers and the IRA used international networks to raise funds (and smuggle weapons), their fights were contained to specific regions. Narco-terrorists in Colombia were able to buy expensive equipment and even compete with the best that American drug enforcement officials had to offer. Nevertheless, their goal was still limited to smuggling drugs. Today, the scope of most lethal organizations is not so limited. In fact, al Qaeda (which means "the base") is not really a particular organization but a loose affiliation of terrorist groups that have common objectives and global ambitions.

One group affiliated with al Qaeda is Jemaah Islamiyah, whose particular objective is to establish an Islamic empire (Daulah Islamiyah) across all of Southeast Asia. While the bulk of recent terrorist incidents have been in Iraq, there is no denying that since September 11, 2001, Malaysia, Singapore, Indonesia, southern Thailand, and the Philippines have all experienced an increase in terrorist activities. Traditionally, this is a region where Muslims have been very moderate, but the rise of radical Wahhabism (an Islamic sect), along with

Saudi money for missions and education, has led to a significant increase in sympathy for radical groups among certain segments of the Muslim world.

In the case of Ayman al Zawahiri and Osama bin Laden, the desire is to remove U.S. troops from Saudi Arabia, establish an Islamic caliphate stretching from Asia to Africa, and destroy capitalism in the process. (Remember, the first two targets on September 11, 2001, were the two towers of the World Trade Center, and the teachings of Islamist hero Sayyid Qutb clearly condemn capitalism.) The battle against al Qaeda has taken international police forces to every continent except Antarctica. The implications of this are huge. While it is highly unlikely that terrorists will ever succeed in their delusional goals, they most certainly have the power to destabilize many countries in the attempt.

Second, aside from their more ambitious goals, today's terrorists are able to poison the well on many different levels because of their global goals. The war against terror has not always been prosecuted in the most effective way, but we must realize that this war is not just an effort to stop individual attacks, but rather it is an international effort to close gaps in our international systems that allow terrorists to flourish.

Terrorism challenges us on many fronts that are not as visible as the carnage of a suicide bomb. Illegal financial transactions and weapon smuggling operations are part of terrorism as well, and a war does need to be waged against these criminal activities because they terrorize and victimize innocent people throughout the world. The terrorist group Jemaah Islamiyah, for instance, set up phony nongovernmental organizations and charities around the world to help fund their work. Furthermore, the methods used by transnational terrorists also pave the way for criminal organizations and drug cartels to avoid detection and subvert the law. Today, the global economy is growing at a phenomenal rate. Disturbingly however, the criminal economy is growing seven times as fast.[1] While the war against terrorism is often reduced to a fight between the West

---

1. John Robb, *Brave New War: The Next Stage of Terrorism and the End of Globalization* (Hoboken, NJ: John Wiley & Sons, 2007), 5.

(particularly the United States) and al Qaeda, the reality is that this is a larger battle between the civilized world and the criminal underworld.

Third, today's weapons of terror are more lethal and less expensive than ever before. While smuggling a suitcase nuke or executing a biological or chemical attack is not easy, make no mistake about it, people are trying to do just that, as William Langewiesche has documented in his book *The Atomic Bazaar*. Yes, it is true that the person reading these words has a much greater chance of dying in a fatal car accident than in a terrorist attack. Even waves of terrorist attacks would not be able to hurt the majority of the population. However, today's attacks can be far more lethal, cause more destruction, damage a greater area in less time, create international tensions, and alter foreign policy—more than ever before. Armed with box cutters and just a few thousand dollars, the 9/11 hijackers were able to kill three thousand people and shift the world geopolitically, costing America and the world billions of dollars.

One of the underreported lessons of the Iraq war is that warfare is becoming more expensive for civil societies and increasingly cheaper and easier for barbarians. In Iraq, soldiers lives are saved by using PackBots which prevent IEDs (improvised explosive devices) from killing soldiers. But each time it takes the bullet for the soldier, the $100,000 PackBot is lost. Meanwhile, the weapon it defuses is made out of a cell phone, garage-door openers, doorbells, and/or a toy's remote control.[2] Thanks to video game technology, GPS devices, Google Earth satellite images and Internet how-to videos, terrorists can not only possess tools that only large well-funded militaries possessed in the past, but now they can also practice open-source warfare comparing techniques, building weapons, and sharing information across borders. Open-source warfare operates a lot like the Linux computer operating system, which has been extended and improved by thousands of programmers around the world sharing information.

In other words, you get more bang for your buck than ever before if you are in the terrorist game. It is because these attacks can be done so easily and effectively on so many different levels of society that there is such a need for vigilance against terrorism.

---

2. Robert M Charette., "Open Source Warfare," Spectrum Online, November 2007, http://spectrum. ieee.org/nov07/5668.

Fourth, today's terrorists are far more educated than the terrorists of the past. Great Britain was shocked to find out, in 2007, that doctors in their health-care system had attempted to carry out terrorist attacks in Scotland and England. Increasingly, doctors, engineers, students at prestigious European universities, and upper- and middle-class youth are among those likely to choose terrorism. Most of them have been educated in the secular ideas of the West, particularly those that are suspicious of capitalism, imperialism, and the foreign policies of countries such as the United States and Israel. In this sense, Osama bin Laden and Ayman al Zawahiri are not too different from the Western-educated tyrants that represented the worst of the Marxist revolutions of the twentieth century.

Many terrorists have attended schools in the West. For instance, Khalid Sheikh Mohammed, who confessed to masterminding the September 11 attacks, the Bali nightclub bombing, and the 1993 World Trade Center bombing, among many other attacks, attended a Baptist school in Murfreesboro, North Carolina, before completing a degree in mechanical engineering at North Carolina Agriculture and Technical State University. Mohammed Atta had a degree from Technical University of Hamburg-Harburg in Germany. Zacarias Moussaoui received flight training in Norman, Oklahoma, and earned a degree in international business from South Bank University in London.

A fifth difference is that negotiations are not an option for Islamic fascists. Unlike the IRA, ETA, or even the Tamil Tigers with their clear objectives, some militant Islamic organizations hope to usher in the apocalypse, or at least achieve

> Most terrorist groups do not care if the whole world goes down with them.

the unachievable—a peaceful pan-Islamic world. With such groups, negotiations are pointless. And due to their decentralized and individualistic natures, there is no one to negotiate with anyway. In the past, the enemy was another country, kingdom, or tribe, and the goals were limited. Even the use of atomic weapons on Hiroshima and Nagasaki by the United States had a goal: to end the fighting quickly. The cold war, in which thousands of nuclear missiles were pointed at specific locations around the world, had a goal as well: to deter the enemy and keep the war from turning hot. A hotline was even set up between the general secretary of the Soviet Union and the president of the United States in case tensions reached crisis level.

Today, most terrorist groups do not care if the whole world goes down with them. Unlike the presidents, dictators, and generals of the past, these groups are not accountable to anyone, even if they bring destruction on their own people. Even Mao Zedong, with his indifference toward the suffering of his people, was ultimately reined in after the disastrous Cultural Revolution. The war-weary Soviets had many nuclear weapons but had no desire to use them, and they still had many citizens to take care of in one way or another. Today's Islamic fascists can hardly wait to use nuclear weapons, and they will not need to justify their actions to anyone afterward. Death and destruction are the glorious goals in and of themselves.

Our Fragile World

The battle against terrorism will continue at the state level with the governments of countries cooperating and mobilizing to prevent the growth of transnational terrorism. Those of us living in the civilized world are tempted to not take these things seriously. Our bubble of civilization creates a perception that the modern world is invulnerable to attack. We have also had so much success in leaving large-scale wars behind that we tend to think everything can be worked out with just the right amount of effort. But the world is far more fragile than we are willing to accept, and the kind of stability we have enjoyed for the past few decades is rare in human history and unlikely to last indefinitely. It would be unrealistic to think that the new lethal possibilities will not be explored on a large scale, if only because there is evil in this world.

As for globalization, the past two periods of hyperglobalization were interrupted by war. Our hope is that this one will not be interrupted by large-scale wars between nations, but it is likely that a significant disruption will occur at some point, just as it has in the past. The attacks of September 11, 2001, were probably a warning that the next disruption will be built on a different platform from what we are expecting—using many of globalization's good things against us.

Despite the fact that globalization is creating many winners, if only 5 percent or 10 percent of the world feels disenfranchised, they can become a significant audience for demagogues preaching a fantasy ideology aimed at overthrowing the global order. Islamic fascism has been the only potent movement against globalization thus far, but it is too early to tell whether it has staying power. Future threats may come from Hindu fundamentalists, nonreligious groups, or nationalistic groups that gravitate towards unrealistic ideological or religious messages of global homogenization. While we don't know who the messengers will be or what form the message will take, there will be more lethal ideologies in the future that attempt to compete with globalization.

As Christians, our primary responsibility, however, is not to worry about what might happen in the future but to have a positive impact in the name of Christ in the here and now. We should be aware that the world is more precarious and fallen than we would like to believe, but we should use that sobering knowledge to spend our days on earth redemptively engaging our communities and being a force for good. In the past, groups preaching hatred have preyed upon those feeling marginalized. Religious communities, more than any other force, can offer hope, love, and support to those feeling displaced. Unfortunately, they can also channel people's energies into negative forms of expression and toward hatred and intolerance. It is vital that we as Christians reach out with a message of truth, hope, and salvation so that negative and false ideologies can be seen for what they are: mere fantasy.

10
consider the jatrophas
of the field

We should care about the environment more than anybody.

> *God-given dominion is a sacred responsibility*
> *to steward the earth and not a license to*
> *abuse the creation of which we are a part.*
>
> National Association of Evangelicals

THE DEBATE OVER global warming is heating up, no pun intended. On one side, some scientists (and Nobel laureate Al Gore) argue that the evidence is indisputable: polar caps are melting, regional climates are changing, and even the animal kingdom is showing signs of strain. And furthermore, they argue, the consensus of scientists believing in global warming is too large to be ignored. It is their opinion that we have to act now to save the environment and that it may already be too late.

Other scientists, though, argue that the earth has actually been cooling for the past few years, that fluctuations are common, and that if we can't trust our local weatherman to be right about the weather on Saturday, how can we possibly think that we can know what will happen fifty years from now? On the skeptical side, the best-known figure is Bjørn Lomborg, who argues that much of the concern about deforestation, lack of oil, and overpopulation is overblown and does not hold up to scrutiny, and that global warming itself is not nearly the pressing issue it is made out to be by scientists and the media.

And Michael Crichton, the author of *Jurassic Park* and creator of *ER*, slams the idea of consensus altogether. In a widely discussed 2005 speech to the National Press Club, this Harvard-educated medical doctor and award-winning author and filmmaker argued: "Consensus is invoked only in situations where the science is not solid enough. Nobody says the consensus of scientists agrees that E=mc². Nobody says the consensus is that the sun is 93 million miles away."[1] Crichton feels that in the past and the present, the sensationalistic nature of the media combined with the politicization of science has led to myths such as extraterrestrial obsession in the 1960s, nuclear winter in the 1970s, and now global warming. He also points out that consensus led to the misdiagnosis of many severe diseases throughout history.

Cause for Concern?

Is the increasingly strange weather a sign that we really are entering a dangerous warming period? Or are we being caught up in a manufactured, political firestorm? And for those of us who never liked science class very much, how can we ever know which side is right?

Fortunately for Christians, the climate debate is mostly a moot point. As Pastor Rob Bell has pointed out, the environment is not a liberal issue; it is a Genesis 1 issue. When I was growing up in the 1970s, we weren't too concerned about littering. But then we were exposed to the famous commercial of a Native American with a tear in his eye as he contemplated the polluting of the land. It was an incredibly effective, guilt-inducing ad. The 1980s followed with a heavy push on recycling and raising environmental consciousness, and my attitude shifted: littering became a cardinal sin. The change in the global psyche about the importance of the environment has been a very positive development.

In general, there is reason to believe that as the world develops and technology becomes more sophisticated, we will avoid the kind of poisonous conditions that accompanied the Industrial Revolution and the lack of concern and inefficiency that was so pervasive in the Eastern Bloc during the cold war. With higher standards of living, more open societies, spreading entrepreneurialism, and a world that is not only more environmentally conscious but also perpetually monitored by numerous watchdog groups, the future will most likely be cleaner than the present.

1. Michael Crichton, "The Case for Skepticism on Global Warming." Speech given to the National Press Club in Washington, DC, on January 25, 2005, http://www.michaelcrichton.net/speech-ourenvironmentalfuture.html.

There is cause for concern, however. The rapid rise in living standards in the emerging nations is increasing the world's demand for energy. China and India, in particular, will not only continue to produce many poorly regulated factories, but they will also create hundreds of millions of new consumers. Already, China's newfound love affair with the automobile is cause for concern. The earth does need to become cleaner as quickly as possible. It is also disturbing to note that much of the world's oil, on which the world is currently dependent for energy, is produced in highly unstable places, such as Venezuela, Nigeria, Iran, and Saudi Arabia.

The toxicity of the land, seas, and skies is also threatening to make some parts of the world uninhabitable. Today, seven of the ten most-polluted cities in the world are in China. Air pollution from China has been discovered as far away as Boston. One-third of the particulate matter hanging in the Los Angeles air comes from China. It is not only China, but also India, Russia, and the other rapidly developing countries of the world that are producing pollutants and suffering the most immediate consequences. Land, water, and the lungs of children are being destroyed, and this is something that will require immediate action.

We have a new class of citizens around the world: environmental refugees.

We live in Hong Kong, where for the past few years we have seen our lungs take a beating. I suffer from a chronic cough, and the doctor tells me that even though I never suffered from any kind of asthma before, I have now moved up the asthma scale. In some neighborhoods here, 60 percent of the children suffer from asthma. The poorly regulated factories of the Pearl River Delta belch filth into the sky that reaches us in Hong Kong, and there is very little that Hong Kong can do about it. Fortunately, the Chinese government is trying to raise environmental standards. Living in certain cities and towns in China has become a death sentence; soil and water are so contaminated that they are causing deformities and terrible premature deaths. As the result of pollution and environmental damage, we have a new class of citizens around the world: environmental refugees. These are people that are forced to leave their homes because they have become uninhabitable due to pollution, development, or environmental calamities. Living in China, we worry about our healthy son and the coughs that seem to linger too long. But even in Europe and North America, asthma rates are increasing dramatically.

It is easy to assign blame to India and China, who are building factories at record speed and creating a new class of consumers who will all want to own cars and other polluting luxury items. But for decades the West has been able to pollute freely; concern in the West for the environment has emerged only recently, and conveniently at a point in time when we have the wealth and technology to support projects that create environmentally efficient products. In much of the emerging world, people are just now, for the first time, able to consume items that the West has enjoyed for decades and they are being asked to severely curtail their consumption right off the bat. It is unfair, but it is necessary—for the sake of the citizens in those emerging nations, if nothing else.

Ingenious Solutions

The amount of pollutants and waste produced by a wealthier, more populated world could be dangerously high. The good news is that the same wealth and large population will drive innovation and give us some ingenious solutions. Military organization may be primarily associated in our minds with war, death, and destruction, but the Defense Advanced Research Projects Agency, the research branch of the U.S. Department of Defense, has funded development of technology that will produce water out of thin air in almost any location in the world.[2]

We may still need oil, but with new technology, we could need far less of it.

Lack of access to clean water is one of the largest causes of disease in the least developed countries, and water scarcity threatens the development of emerging nations, China and India in particular. Such technology will also be incredibly helpful in responding to natural disasters.

The Boeing company, which produces, among many other things, commercial aircraft, has recently unveiled the 787 Dreamliner. This unique plane

---

2. Audrey Hudson, "Making Water from Thin Air," *Wired Magazine*, October 6, 2006, http://www.wired.com/science/discoveries/news/2006/10/71898.

will be capable of flying very long distances, yet it will burn 20 percent less fuel than jetliners of similar size. This is because the plane is made of carbon-fiber composites. The use of light metals and ultra light steels means the planes are just as strong as, if not stronger than, the older models, but they make the plane lighter and require less fuel. With every major airline company in the world signing up to buy the new plane, it became the fastest-selling wide body in history; there is now an eight-year waiting list for delivery. Ford Motor Company has taken an interest in the plane's success and hopes to make cars out of light metals that will be safer and far more economical than the ones currently used. This technology could reduce both fatal car accidents and the demand for oil. We may still need oil for the next three decades, but with new technology, we could need far less of it.

In Australia, a company called Solar Systems is creating photovoltaic power stations that produce electricity directly from the effect of photons striking semi-conducting materials. Solar power has long been hampered by its inefficient energy conversion, but this new technology turns sunlight into electricity at the same efficiency as burning coal. Increasingly, the obstacles to alternative energy sources are disappearing. And not only are new energy sources becoming more efficient and cost effective, but the technology is also more portable, as is the case with many new solar products; this will benefit least developed countries, which often do not have much electrical power but have plenty of sunlight.

Many of the emerging nations are trying to get on top of this crisis and are making significant contributions of their own. Brazil has been a leader in the use of sugar cane to produce ethanol. China, India, and some African nations are cultivating the jatropha tree, which produces massive amounts of oil that can be used to produce nontoxic biodiesel. The results have been very promising so far, and the jatropha can be grown on over half of the African continent. Thus far, tests show that it is far more efficient than other alternative fuels, including ethanol. And it is approaching commercialization rapidly. Other radical innovations are in the pipeline.

One of the great benefits of the environmental challenge is that not only is it forcing cleaner, technological innovations, but it is also fostering coop-eration and shared responsibility between countries. The more that science and technology is shared between countries such as China, India, and the United States, the greater chances there are for peace. Mutual dependence for a common cause is a unifying force, and a higher consciousness about the planet's beauty reduces the likelihood of the kind of large-scale state-on-state wars seen in the nineteenth and twentieth centuries.

Christian Responses

Christians have, in general, been slow to get involved in the environmental movement because of concerns about hidden political agendas, contradictory facts, and the pantheistic worldview of some environmentalists. But Christians should be the first to fight for a cleaner world—it is our Father who created it for us. We Christians have to be careful not to let the politicized nature of the environmental debate lead us to disengage.

Blame and ignorance is not something we can afford in this fight. There is not enough time. The world may or may not be getting warmer, but the effect of two billion people entering the global workforce and raising their standards of living is going to strain the global environment—that much is assured. It is happening right now. Furthermore, the existing lack of clean water around the world and the depletion of fisheries are two issues that have consistently rated as major environmental threats equal to or greater than global warming.

Fortunately, evangelicals are increasingly embracing environmentalism (or "creation care," as it is sometimes called)—for theological reasons instead of political ones. In 2004, the National Association of Evangelicals adopted the "Evangelical Call to Civic Responsibility," which called for evangelicals to "labor to protect God's creation."[3] On the interfaith front, Greenfaith is an organization that, among many other things, trains Christian organizations and leaders to be environmental leaders.[4]

An incredible variety of Christian organizations are mobilizing believers for creation care—that is caring for the earth and being a part of Christ's act of reconciliation with creation. The Evangelical Environmental Network is one such organization that assists individuals, families, and churches to become environmentally conscious. In addition to publishing a quarterly titled

---

3. National Association of Evangelicals, "For the Health of the Nation: An Evangelical Call to Civic Responsibility," National Association of Evangelicals, October 2004, http://www.nae.net/images/civic_responsibility2.pdf.

4. www.greenfaith.org

Creation Care, the EEN has also created a kit of materials, "Let the Earth Be Glad," to help churches explore a biblical approach to caring for the environment. The kit includes information on how churches can manage their church buildings and church grounds in a more energy efficient way, as well as providing pastors with theological information upon which to build the biblical case for caring for the environment.[5]

Floresta, another Christian organization, develops innovative ways to get Christian individuals and churches involved in environmental and development issues. Projects currently include attempts to reverse deforestation and alleviate poverty in rural areas of the world. Deforestation occurs when forested areas are converted to other uses, including agriculture, urban development, or other forms of land development. It can upset the biodiversity of the land, displace people, change the local weather, and strip the forests of their trees. In many developing nations, farmers lose valuable land and economic opportunities. Floresta invites church teams and Christian individuals to plant trees, provide micro-loans, sponsor a village, and even get involved in agroforestry projects.[6] Target Earth, another Christian agency, provides short-term mission experiences. It focuses on endangered land, reforestation, feeding the hungry, and saving the jaguar from extinction.[7]

> **We Christians have to be careful not to let the politicized nature of the environmental debate lead us to disengage.**

Each one of these Christian organizations invites Christians to tackle the huge environmental challenges in small but effective ways. Small efforts can make a significant difference in this struggle to clean the earth. Both Christian and secular organizations and companies are making great efforts at rising to that challenge.

There are many reasons for Christians to not turn their backs on environmental concerns. But the greatest is simply that examining the environment is ultimately an examination of God's goodness. In the story of the jatropha tree, we see the great complexity of nature as well as the stunning innovation

---

5. www.creationcare.org

6. www.floresta.org

7. www.targetearth.org

unleashed by the human mind. Both are products of his creation, and both are magnificent to behold. Our environmental crisis is really an opportunity to shine the light on God's glory. This is the real meaning of having dominion over the earth. Consider the lilies indeed!

11
russians come in
from the cold

Beware of underpopulation.

*Whoever does not miss the Soviet Union has
no heart. Whoever wants it back has no brain.*

Vladimir Putin

IN 1985, WE waved goodbye with trepidation to my sister Marcel as she went
off to study Russian in the Soviet Union. The cold war was still being waged,
and we in the West had grown up fearing the atheistic Soviets. My sister managed to survive her time in Moscow and Leningrad, and she even managed to
smuggle in a Bible and smuggle out a Komsomol uniform and an enormous
Soviet flag. It was a dangerous thing to do, but she made it back to us in one
piece. It was that very spring that Mikhail Gorbachev became the general secretary of the Communist Party and ushered in changes that would ultimately
exacerbate the disintegration of the Soviet Union. The Eastern superpower
was super no more.

The Wild, Wild East

It has been less than twenty years since the collapse of the Soviet Union
and the rise of the new Russia. Initially, there was anticipation that Russia's
transition into the free world would go as smoothly as it had for some of the
Eastern Bloc nations. Russia's new leader, Boris Yeltsin, befriended Bill Clinton,
and some had high hopes that the country could quickly become a Western-
style democracy. But Americans and many others misread the situation. The
transition to democracy requires healthy institutions, the rule of law, sound
fiscal management, security, a relatively well-educated population, and high

levels of trust. Russia had a highly educated population, but the economic shock-therapy measures recommended by the West, as well as some of the deeper cultural and historical issues, led to a great divide between rich and poor, the looting of many of the State's most valuable assets, and the collapse of the banking system. Crime and corruption exploded, eroding the people's trust, which already was low under the Soviet system. Through the 1990s, the predictability of the old Soviet age gave way to a new age that looked more like the wild, wild West of the nineteenth-century United States. Indeed, it was even called the "Wild East" for a time. Footage of terrorist bombings, assassinations, the rise of the mafia, and two ferocious wars waged in Chechnya filled our TV screens.

Despite many newfound freedoms, the new Russia is, for many, a more discouraging place to live than it was two decades ago. When I visited Moscow for the first time in 2007, I wanted to ask Russians about their opinions of life in the new Russia; I wanted to be sensitive, though. I didn't even have to ask. A mere five minutes into the ride from the airport, our driver was telling us stories about how difficult life was now compared to the old days when the check was guaranteed to be in the mail and the money went farther than it does now. The sense of discontent is great, particularly among the older generation, many of whom spent years toiling under the Soviet system only to find themselves now living in a country where a monthly pension of sixty dollars will barely cover the cost of a meal in a nice restaurant.

Russia's homicide rate is twenty times that of Western Europe, and many of the murders involve contract killings.[1] In the old days, it is was impossible to do anything without the permission of the Communist Party; today, it is difficult for businesses, and even churches, to get anything done without dealing with the powerful Russian mafia. In most countries, criminal organizations are limited to extortion, drugs, prostitution, and gambling. In Russia, the mafia have far greater rein and even meddle in the affairs of churches. The police are often just as corrupt as the mafia (and less admired). Doing business is not easy in Russia, and it has stunted the development of small businesses, which has hurt the economy. Extortion extinguishes entrepreneurialism.

---

1. *The Economist*, "Dangerous Russia: Fools and Bad Roads, *The Economist*, May 22· 2007, http://www.economist.com/displayStory.cfm?story_id=8896844.

A Dying Population

Life is fragile in Russia. Work fatalities, driving fatalities, and suicides are much more common than in most emerging nations and developed nations. Life expectancies are surprisingly short. The rate for men under the age of sixty-five dying a violent death is a dozen times higher than in the United Kingdom. Even more unusual is that the death rate for women is higher than for most Western European men. As an emerging nation, Russia's life expectancy is closer to that of a least developed country, another reminder that emerging nations may have fast-growing economies and generate a lot of wealth but still have serious third-world problems. The U.S. Census Bureau estimates that life expectancy for Russian men over the next two decades will be at the level of least developed countries Bangladesh and Pakistan. In the year 2000, a twenty-year-old Russian had only a 46 percent chance of surviving to reach age sixty-five (the figure was 79 percent for American youth).[2]

> We have spent decades worrying about overpopulation, but the real threat in the future is more likely to be underpopulation.

Even if we allow for the improved economic situation to improve the mortality rates, it doesn't change the fact that for many in Russia, deeply ingrained cultural habits can be hard to break, and more money may make them worse. Many who escape violent death or sickness simply drink themselves to death; alcohol remains an enormous problem in a country known for its vodka. For example, in one Russian city, 43 percent of all deaths from 2003 to 2005 of men aged twenty-five to fifty-four were directly attributable to alcohol.[3]

Russia has a dying population, meaning that there are more people dying each year than being born, and that situation is even more challenging than overpopulation. When demographic decline occurs on this scale, it is very difficult for a country to turn it around and survive—and even less likely that it can gain (or retain) world power status. Shockingly, many of Russia's

---

2. Nicholas Eberstadt, "Russia: The Sick Man of Europe," American Enterprise Institute for Public Policy Research, January 1, 2005, http://www.aei.org/publications/filter.all,publD.21711/pub_detail.asp.

3. Reuters, Alcohol-Related Deaths High for Men in Russia, June 15, 2007, http://www.reuters.com/article/healthNews/idUSPAR55315420070615.

deaths are preventable. Part of the problem is the issue of low fertility rates, a problem plaguing many nations.

We have spent decades worrying about overpopulation, but the real threat in the future is more likely to be *under*population. Many of the world's wealthiest countries, including Singapore, Japan, and most of Western Europe, are facing an aging crisis. In 2000, at 15 percent, Europe had the highest percentage of people aged sixty-five years or older. That number is expected to double by 2050.[4] Japan's situation is worse: by 2050, nearly 44 percent of the population will be over the age of sixty.[5] In Italy, there are 103 deaths for every 100 births. That is an alarming statistic and bodes poorly for Italy. In Russia, however, there are 160 deaths for every 100 births. From 1991 to 2004, there were ten million more burials in Russia than births.[6] For a country that is in an era of peace and economic improvement, this is quite extraordinary.

The situation is not limited to the wealthy nations of East Asia and the Western world. Poor countries in Africa face steep declines due to HIV deaths; life expectancies in some African nations have dropped to as low as thirty years. The populations of the central Asian republics and Eastern Europe are also in decline, and by 2050, even Latin America will have a population of which 19 percent is over the age of sixty-five.[7]

Governments are trying a variety of techniques to get people to have more children, including matchmaking services (Singapore), speed dating (Japan), financial incentives (Germany), and, in one Russian province, giving couples time off from work on an annual "conception day."[8] Allowing immigration is one solution, but the countries with the most pressing aging problems—Italy, Germany, Russia, and Japan—are all quite hostile to the idea of letting in so many immigrants.

4. Kevin Kinsella and Victoria A. Velkoff, *An Aging World: 2001,* Series P95/01-1, (Washington, DC: U.S. Census Bureau, 2001), 9, http://www.census.gov/prod/2001pubs/p95-01-1.pdf.

5. *Foreign Policy*, "The List: Five Population Trends to Watch," *Foreign Policy,* September 2007, http://www.foreignpolicy.com/story/cms.php?story_id=3981.

6. Eberstadt, "Russia, the Sick Man of Europe."

7. Population statistics and discussions are readily available. The Population Reference Bureau (www.prb.org) is an excellent online source. See also Philip Longman, *The Empty Cradle: How Falling Birthrates Threaten World Prosperity and What to Do about It* (New York: Basic Books, 2004); Ben J. Wattenberg, *Fewer: How the New Demography of Depopulation Will Shape Our Future* (Chicago: Ivan R. Dee, 2004).

8. *Foreign Policy*, "The List: Five Population Trends to Watch."

Both Russia and China, as emerging nations that are seeing rapid economic growth after years of poverty, are facing populations that are aging too rapidly. A shrinking workforce can reduce productivity while demanding more support for pension and social welfare systems. Health-care costs and the lack of large families to care for elderly parents will also be a great source of trouble for many nations in the future; they already threaten the newly found success of Russia and China. Both of those emerging nations have very little time to turn things around.

In Russia, the declining population has been caused, in part, by the high rate of abortions. As a result of damage from abortions, many Russian women suffer from infertility. The rate of abortions is still five times that of the United States and is fourth in the world, behind Vietnam, Cuba, and Romania.[9] A Russian woman has more abortions than births over the course of her childbearing years. In 2002, the country recorded 1.7 million abortions—more than 120 for every 100 live births.[10] Russians are now choosing to have smaller families; some have no choice due to infertility.

During the Soviet era, abortions were the primary method of birth control.

Making matters worse are venereal diseases, TB, and an AIDS epidemic that is considered one of the world's most serious. AIDS in Russia is mostly the result of infected needles used by drug users. It was only in 2007 that the government finally established the Government Commission on AIDS, but it will be a challenge to implement policies in a country that is now very decentralized and that suffers from a weak medical infrastructure, which itself is a contributing factor to Russia's unusually high rates of tuberculosis. It currently ranks twelfth out of twenty-two countries that have high rates of tuberculosis and strains of TB that are increasingly drug resistant.[11] As for

---

9. "Russians Feel Abortions Complications: Used as Birth Control in Soviet Times Practice Has Led to Widespread Complications," *Washington Post*, February 22, 2003, A16.

10. Eberstadt, "Russia, the Sick Man of Europe."

11. USAID, "Russia: Tuberculosis Profile," September 2006, http://www.usaid.gov/our_work/global_health/id/tuberculosis/countries/eande/russia.pdf.

venereal diseases, in 2001, the number of people in Russia with syphilis was forty times higher than in Germany.[12]

Also affecting Russia are the new attitudes toward marriage and divorce. Divorce has become more common in the new Russia. In 1990, before the collapse of the Soviet Union, the divorce rate was roughly 40 percent. By 1995, the odds of divorce had risen to 50 percent.[13] More liberal attitudes, women in the workforce, and delaying marriage may have long-term effects on the country, keeping birthrates too low.

While there are signs of increased birthrates in certain parts of Russia, the fastest foreseeable way to reverse this dying trend is through immigration. Currently, many Muslims from the former Soviet republics are choosing to settle in Russia, making it the second most popular destination for immigrants in the world after the United States. This, however, has led to an increase in racism and xenophobia. Furthermore, as a recent RAND Europe study shows, immigration may not be enough to solve the problems of a dying population.[14]

For some in Russia, however, life has never been better, but it comes at the cost of a huge divide between rich and poor. Today, instead of the small private dachas of elite party members dotting the landscape on the outskirts of Moscow, there are now entire neighborhoods whose homes surpass even those of Beverly Hills. Russia is also a land of billionaires, and Moscow is now consistently rated the most expensive city in the world for expatriates. A cup of coffee can cost more than in notoriously pricey Tokyo.

Christianity in Russia

The openness toward evangelical Christianity so prevalent after the collapse of the Soviet Union has declined substantially. It is more difficult for evangelical missionaries and churches to be heard when they have to compete against the flood of ideas and products that globalization is bringing to Russia. Nevertheless, the Russian people have always been a deeply spiritual

---

12. Eberstadt, "Russia, the Sick Man of Europe."

13. Ibid.

14. Jonathan Grant et al, *Low Fertility and Population Ageing: Causes, Consequences, and Policy Options*, monograph prepared for the European Commission (Cambridge, UK: RAND Europe, 2004), http://www.rand.org/pubs/monographs/2004/RAND_MG206.pdf.

people—but in a more Eastern mystical way instead of the West's more rational approach to faith.

Christianity's imprint on the Russian soul is strong. That imprint, however, has been formed by one thousand years of Christianity as interpreted by the Russian Orthodox Church. This can be a very tricky environment for evangelical missions. There is great familiarity with institutional Christianity but not much understanding of a personal relationship with Christ. An evangelical view of Christianity is likely to get you labeled as a cult. Most Russian Orthodox priests would no more want to cooperate with evangelicals than most evangelicals would want to worship God in the Mormon Tabernacle in Salt Lake City. Relations have been further strained by the sometimes culturally insensitive way that evangelical organizations moved into Russia after the collapse of the Soviet Union—oblivious to the fact that Christianity had been in Russia for a millennium and that many in the church had suffered great persecution for their faith.

The openness toward evangelical Christianity in Russia has declined substantially.

The physical and spiritual terrain of Russia is very difficult to navigate for those who want to stay true to the gospel. It may well be one of the most difficult mission fields in the world. Slavic culture, a painful bloody history, corruption in the Russian Orthodox Church, the gap between rich and poor, the rapid influx of new ideas, general distrust, and the culturally ingrained sense of fatalism—all of these make it very difficult for the liberating gospel to take root. Fortunately, the Russian church has some outstanding congregations in Russia, and you could not hope to meet a more loving and wonderfully committed people anywhere in the world.

I recently visited a congregation in Chelyabinsk and was truly humbled by the people's warm spirit and commitment in the face of challenges that very few of us on the mission field have to face. Challenges and obstacles surround the Russian church at all times. It is never easy for them. But through their commitment to each other and to Christ, they are bringing the warmth of *agape*-love to a place that has been in a deep freeze for a very long time.

The Russians are in the habit of looking at Orthodox icons in order to catch a glimpse of heaven. The paintings are beautiful, but they cannot compete with the living icon of a church that serves and meets people right where they are in life. Our Russian brothers and sisters are trying to make those Jesus paintings come to life for the people in their country.

Looking Forward

We shouldn't expect emerging nations like Russia and China to look like the United States anytime soon. The United States of America has had a two-hundred-year head start on democracy and has been blessed, more than almost any other nation, with an unusually advantageous combination of history, geography, demographics, and natural resources. Russia is a completely different animal. Nevertheless, this should not frighten us from getting to know Russia and her people. Even some of Russia's more antagonistic positions with regard to the West have more to do with the countries sharing its borders (particularly in Central Asia) than it does with the West itself. Geographically speaking, Russia, with its large and mostly unpopulated borders, is vulnerable; it already faces an "invasion" of Chinese immigrants working Russian land along its southern borders.

Currently, President Vladimir Putin is attempting to recentralize Russia and banking the country's future on natural resources like oil. Traditionally, this has been a recipe for disaster. When the wealth and development of a country are dependent on a commodity like oil, it discourages broader development. And when the country has a long history of corruption and apathy, the chances of a commodity like oil truly helping people at all levels of society decreases significantly. However, Putin has also shown himself to be highly intelligent and very aware of Russia's history, culture, and limitations as it seeks to integrate better with the West. Russia, like China, will continue to be misunderstood by the countries of the West, none of which share Russia's unique and tragic history. As for Putin, he is most likely a transitional figure buying time for the country as it attempts to develop the institutions and national character necessary for a healthy civil society. Putin runs what amounts to a multiethnic empire where the people are not familiar with the concept of individual rights but are used to and often prefer autocratic rule.

Despite the huge challenge of demographic decline, there is some good news coming out of Russia. Russians have relatively free access to the Internet, and millions are seeing an improvement in their standard of living. Vladimir

Putin has, at times, played upon nationalistic feelings and the ancient Russian tradition of a strong central leader, but he has also ushered in some much-needed reforms, such as land reform and a flat tax. The economy is doing better, and the government has even started building foreign reserves. And of course, we must remember that America, the most-commonly imitated democracy, took decades of sometimes painful change to truly transform into the country that it is today.

What is clear is that many Russians today are hurting. The statistics are not just numbers, but people. There are Russians in prison with TB in need of visitation (which Pastor Andrei in Chelyabinsk does at great risk to his own health). There are women who carry the physical and emotional scars of abortion. There are drug users suffering from AIDS and wasting away on the streets or in impoverished medical facilities. There are senior citizens barely able to get by each month and suffering from a lifetime of disillusionment. And there are those who are making the tragic mistake of expecting wealth to solve everything.

Emerging nations like Russia and China won't look like the United States anytime soon.

It is cold in Russia, and the winter has been long. While the global markets ponder whether it is safe to invest in Russia, we Christians must invest ourselves there. Our churches and mission organizations need to do all we can to help the people of this great land. If Jesus were walking on the earth today, he would be running, not walking, to lay his warm healing hands on the broken people of the cold north.

12
focus on
the city

Urbanization is remaking our world.

*Our ability to affect events is limited. Moreover,
each place has a life of its own that an
individual mayor can influence but rarely alter.*

Daniel Kemmis
former mayor of Missoula, Montana

I HAVE ALWAYS loved cities. As a child, I used to enjoy looking up statistics on the world's most populous metropolitan areas. Year after year, the cities were always the same: Tokyo, Mexico City, New York, and so on. These major urban centers were well-known throughout the world. But something began to happen in the late 1980s: the names on the list began to change and become less familiar. Kinshasa, Dhaka, Lagos, Chongqing, and São Paulo made the list, and New York's thirteen million people suddenly seemed small in comparison. What happened? One word: urbanization.

In the past twenty years, the world has experienced incredible demographic changes. People are migrating to cities in mass numbers. Congo (DR), Bangladesh, Nigeria, China, and Brazil are just a few of the nations that have seen millions leave the countryside to look for opportunities in the city. China currently has a floating population of two hundred million migrant workers looking for work in China's largest urban areas. It is the largest peacetime migration in human history. Overall, half the world's population (approximately, three billion out of six billion) now lives in a major metropolitan area; in a few decades, the proportion of urban-dwellers will rise to two-thirds.[1] Cities like

---

1. Mike Davis, *Planet of Slums* (London: Verso, 2006), 2.

Chicago that once seemed so large are now tiny in comparison to the world's megacities (populations greater than eight million) and hypercities (populations greater than twenty million).

Globalization is creating great challenges for rural and agrarian areas. In order to profit under globalization, people must have access to infrastructure and technology. Such factors as regular electricity, functional roads, airports, access to computers, and an educated and skilled population make cities attractive to global investors. Agrarian life is increasingly a low-paying, difficult way of life. Emerging nations like China are moving away from agriculture to manufacturing, while developed nations like the United States and Japan are moving from manufacturing to a service economy and high-tech industry.

Overall, urbanization is part of a good trend. The world's standard of living is rising through economic development. But it is also putting a strain on cities as more and more people position themselves in urban areas to take advantage of economic opportunities. Unfortunately, for many of the migrants moving to cities in least developed countries like the Democratic Republic of Congo and Bangladesh, jobs can often be scarce, low paying, or nonexistent. One of the problems is that many of the least developed countries suffer from the unfair agricultural trade practices of Western nations like France and the United States, which increases the number of migrants looking for work in the city. When wealthier countries subsidize their farmers and impose tariffs on agricultural imports, it artificially lowers the price of their own domestic crops and increases the price of imports; as a result, the poorer LDC farmer is priced out of the global market. With no hope of breaking through the global trade barriers, many rural farmers migrate to the city.

An Unprecedented Event

A common theme throughout this book is the speed and scale at which the changes connected with globalization are taking place. While the world has experienced periods of urbanization before, nothing in human history compares to the current migration to cities. We are moving rapidly toward a situation the world has never seen before—a primarily urbanized population.

The success of a country's cities is often a mark of its overall ability to provide for its people. Germany, the United States, and Japan are examples of developed nations with multiple healthy large cities that are able to function extremely well by global standards. And in surveys that measure the livability of cities, Zurich, Switzerland; Vancouver, Canada; and Melbourne, Australia consistently rank high. While there may be pockets of poverty and crime in these cities, these urban areas, much like the countries in which they are located in, generally function very well. Meanwhile, LDC cities like Lagos, Nigeria; Karachi, Pakistan; and Dhaka, Bangladesh usually occupy the bottom spots in surveys measuring livability. In many of the emerging nations and least developed countries, urbanization is occurring at such a high rate that the municipal governments cannot provide adequate infrastructure or housing. Hundreds of millions of people today live as squatters in the world's urban centers, and it is the cities in least developed nations and emerging nations that are experiencing population explosions.

Cities are places of extremes. Within them, we find humanity at its most innovative and at its most depraved.

Cities are places of extremes. Within them, we find humanity at its most innovative and at its most depraved. People migrate to cities because of the promise of possibility—and that promise sometimes pays off and brings new opportunities, but it can bring new complications as well. For many migrants, regardless of economic level, moving to the city is disorienting; it requires a complete reorientation to life. This provides great opportunities for Christian ministry; Christians can provide friendship, social services, a place of worship, and ultimately a spiritual center of gravity.

Twenty-First Century Cities

As our world becomes predominantly urban, at least three types of cities will play a vital role in the twenty-first century:

1. Traditional Centers
(e.g., New York, Paris, London, Singapore, Frankfurt, Tokyo)
These well-known cities are no longer the world's largest, but they are the wealthiest and they will wield greater influence via globalization in the future. While they are not growing rapidly due to the fact that urbanization has peaked in developed nations, they nevertheless remain at the center of

global trade, so their influence cannot be underestimated. Cities like London and New York generate more wealth than many least developed nations, such as Chad or Laos. In the 1990s, Orange County (Los Angeles) did more trade than five-sixths of the world's countries.[2] These traditional centers are often more populous than entire nations. Tokyo has slightly more people than Canada and five times as many people as Costa Rica. These modern, successful developed-nation cities have the infrastructure, technology, and experience to keep them at the center of global trade for decades to come.

Christian growth tends to be stagnant in these wealthy cities. The materialism that permeates them takes its toll on the spirit. Some of these cities are located in countries that were once "Christian," but they are now very secular. Churches tend to be small and the evangelical movement insignificant in comparison to rural areas and to many cities in emerging and least developed nations. The exceptions in these secular nations are in the Christian immigrant populations in cities like Paris, London, and Rome.

In the future, the traditional centers will become increasingly interconnected with each other and disconnected from the poorer regions of the world. Already, many large cities are becoming more disconnected from the countries where they are located. One of the more disturbing trends is the tendency for these cities to create a wealthy class of citizens who disconnect from the people around them. One sign of this, particularly in the United States, is urban flight: As populations have exploded, large numbers of people moved to the suburbs. Such cities suffered from overdevelopment and urban sprawl. Houston, Atlanta, and Phoenix are just three examples.

In some of these traditional centers, though, the trend has been for the cost of both rent and home ownership to rise so high that few can afford to live in the center of town. Owning a home in central Sydney, central London, or central Tokyo would get you a mansion just about anywhere else in the world. Apartments are not much better. Rents in central Hong Kong can be as high as $40,000 (U.S.) a month. The result is that increasingly an elite class of citizens occupies the downtown areas of these traditional centers. They are likely to be wealthy, well-educated, and plugged into the globalized world.

---

2. Robert D. Kaplan, *An Empire Wilderness: Travels into America's Future* (New York: Vintage Books, 1999), 97.

Not just anyone can afford to pack up and move to London, Boston, or Seattle anymore.

Within these traditional centers, technology is making it possible for companies to base themselves in the suburbs rather than downtown. Olathe, on the Kansas side of Kansas City, is one such place: Numerous large and wealthy companies have set up shop in industrial parks and commercial areas. The result is a fast-growing, booming suburb. Technology is also enabling more people to work from home, which is also having an effect on these cities. In contrast to least developed countries or emerging nations, good-paying opportunities can be found without leaving your house in developed countries.

Traditional urban centers will become increasingly interconnected with each other and disconnected from the poorer regions of the world.

It is a sign of great prosperity that the citizens of these traditional centers can live so well, but it can come at a high cost. Life increasingly becomes about work and the acquisition of things. It is an ironic fact that the wealthy are often less happy and satisfied with life than the poor. Anyone who has ever visited slums can attest to the fact that there is a surprising amount of joy to be found in places of dire poverty. While the poor may not have much, they often have family and community. In traditional centers, two incomes are usually required to make ends meet, and families become smaller. Another cost is the increasing disconnection from nature. We are fortunate that we are not as dependent on nature as the ancients were (or as the people in sub-Saharan Africa are today), but agrarian life has brought a valuable perspective to people over the centuries—a healthy sense that life is fleeting and that we must live in community with the earth and our neighbors.

Some traditional cities have disconnected not only from nature but from their neighbors. In Paris, the low-income suburbs have mostly been isolated and left to fend for themselves. The rise of gated-communities from Manila to Omaha is not only a sign of new security concerns but of a desire to be isolated from other communities that may be poorer and of a different class.

As centers of global technology, innovation, education, and culture, it is vital that we attempt to bring Christ to the influential citizens of these cities. For example, Hong Kong's Christian minority (4 percent) may be small in number, but because of Hong Kong's economic resources and influence throughout the region, they are able to have an enormous impact for Christ in Asia and around the world. Their ability to support Christian media, publications, missions, relief work, and the Christian movement in general far exceeds their numerical size.

At the same time, traditional centers will be the home of the global elite who will be the most tempted to succumb to the secularizing forces of the marketplace and distance themselves from those who are struggling in this new age.

2. New Global Centers
(e.g., Bangkok, São Paulo, Kuala Lumpur, Shanghai, Mumbai, Jakarta, Mexico City, Johannesburg)

For most of my life, the three stock exchanges that the world kept an eye on daily were in New York, Tokyo, and London. These three cities and their markets indicated how well the world was doing economically. Today, these cities have a lot of competition. Hong Kong, Shanghai, and Mumbai (formerly Bombay) are now watched just as closely; at times, Hong Kong has temporarily led the way in IPOs (initial private offerings). Cities like Shanghai and Mumbai, located in emerging nations, are what I call the new global centers.

These cities have a fast-growing emerging middle class that is fueling economic growth. All of these metropolises have grown so quickly in the past fifteen years that they are virtually unrecognizable to people who last visited them in the 1980s. Their populations may or may not have increased significantly, but their skylines have definitely been transformed. The new wealth is clearly visible in towering skyscrapers, large shopping malls, fancy cars, and fashionable dress. Houses in the suburbs of Kuala Lumpur, Malaysia, for instance, are just as fancy as anything that can be found in the United States or Europe. And the middle-class teenagers in cities like São Paulo, Brazil, or Jakarta, Indonesia, are world citizens—hardly distinct from the average American teen.

Nevertheless, these cities are found in countries that are still very poverty-stricken. Bangkok, Thailand, is not only a modern city of five million with shopping malls and fancy business hotels, but it is also a city with poor children swimming and bathing in the polluted Chao Phraya River. Shanghai, China, with a population of eighteen million people, has a new high-speed train, the world's largest port, and four times as many skyscrapers as New York City. However, not only is it filled with millions of migrant workers living in subpar conditions, but the city, built on a drained swamp, is now sinking. In São Paulo, Brazil, another city of skyscrapers as far as the eye can see, there are people so rich they take helicopters to work. Meanwhile, on the outskirts of the city are *favelas* (slums) where people can barely afford a television. Some neighborhoods are run by gangs of children, while others are exclusive gated communities for the elite.

The new global centers are dynamic, but their infrastructure may be inadequate, poorly planned, or built too fast. While large segments of the population are enjoying being plugged into the world and seeing their standards of living rise, equally large percentages are living in squalor. In today's era of globalization, the new global centers like Mumbai, India, are now places where one can live a very comfortable existence in one area of the city with all the same amenities available in the West, while a couple of miles away, people live in a slum with no running water or sewage facilities. Moscow has tens of thousands of dingy Soviet-era apartments all linked to the same heating system, yet it also has suburbs with Connecticut-sized mansions.

> **The new global centers are dynamic, but their infrastructure may be inadequate, poorly planned, or built too fast.**

The new global centers are playing an important part in the world's economic boom since they are usually located in emerging nations and tend to be centers of economic activity in their countries. But they are also cities in transition, undergoing great strain as some reap tremendous benefits and others struggle to keep up. While these cities may have McDonald's, KFC, and even TGI Friday's, they are still struggling to provide basic services for all of their people. For instance, Bangalore has many high-tech firms but no high-tech transportation system, and the city floods during heavy rains. In some cases, these societies have all the material trappings of a developed nation, but as far as the rule of law, legal rights, human rights, and other characteristics of civil society, they are still considerably underdeveloped.

Despite their uneven development, these cities are centers of government, education, economics, and culture in their countries, and that is what draws migrants in from the countryside. These cities wield tremendous influence in the rest of the country. If these cities can be reached for Christ, they will influence the rest of the country. Migrant populations in these cities are in a constant state of flux as people adjust to this new world, as they respond to the forces of globalization. This often leads them to search for spiritual meaning. If migrants accept Christ, they may very well take their faith back to their villages.

3. Disintegrating Cities
(e.g., Lagos, Dhaka, Lima, Kinshasa, Karachi, Cairo, Phnom Penh)

As the world's population becomes more urban, it is these cities that will grow the fastest. In the least developed countries, many choose to move to the cities to find opportunity and escape the hazards of rural life, but they do not always find decent opportunities. Instead, they become unemployed people in cities that are ill-equipped to take care of them. These cities exist in countries whose central governments are already having difficulty governing, and municipal governments are doing no better. As a result, millions live in slums as cities disintegrate into chaos. The Democratic Republic of Congo's government is so weak that it can barely be called a country, and in the capital of Kinshasa, seven million people live in mostly abominable conditions. In Cairo, a city of sixteen million, the so-called City of the Dead is a four-mile-long cemetery that houses nearly a million people—most from slums or transplants from a village. While only 6 percent of the developed world's population lives in slums, the figure is 78 percent for urbanites of least developed countries.[3] To say that this is a crisis is an understatement. This kind of unhealthy urbanization can have catastrophic consequences leading to global pandemics, mass migration, and social instability.

Slums are characterized by overcrowding, poor and informal housing, inadequate access to safe water and sanitation, and insecurity of tenure. The nation with the highest percentage of slum dwellers is Ethiopia, with 99.4 percent of its urban population living in slums. Chad, Afghanistan, and Nepal are just behind that, all with more than 90 percent of urbanites living in slums. The fastest growing slums are in the Russian Federation, and the poorest slum populations are in Luanda, Angola; Maputo, Mozambique; Cochabamba,

---

3. Davis, *Planet of Slums*, 23.

Bolivia; and Kinshasa, Congo.[4] Meanwhile, the largest slums in the world are Neza/Chalco/Izta (Mexico City) with four million slum dwellers; Libertador in Caracas, Venezuela, with 2.2 million people; and El Sur/Ciudad Bolivar in Bogotá, Colombia, which has just over two million living in squalor.[5] Latin America is the continent that is urbanizing the fastest and to the greatest degree, consequently most of its major cities have large numbers of slum dwellers.

While our image of slums may be of people living in tin shacks surrounded by human waste, slums can become cities unto themselves, with an underground economy, and shacks may have landlords. Slums may be run by gangs that provide a form of government; they may have schools, brothels, and churches (most likely Pentecostal). What slums do not have are many legitimate economic opportunities. The worst slums are often located in countries that are either disconnected from the global economy or are just now becoming engaged on a bigger scale. Poor cities like Dhaka, Bangladesh, will attract little investment and little attention compared to other world cities.

> **Slums have high birthrates and few economic opportunities. This is an explosive mix.**

In the future, these disintegrating cities will probably breed more conflict, disease, and poverty given that they are located in countries with high birthrates and few economic opportunities. This is an explosive mix. These populations are open to religion, for better and for worse. Some will turn to hopelessness or fanaticism. The radical Islamic Brotherhood has always done well among Cairo's poor, for instance, since they provide more social services than the actual government. But some will turn to other faiths; slum dwellers will most likely turn to Christianity, more than to any other faith.

India is the nation with the most slums, and many slum-dwellers are Dalits (also known as "untouchables"), who are tired of being marginalized in small villages and come to the city where it is much more difficult to maintain rigid discrimination. Although part of the Hindu caste system, Dalits are turning to Christianity in record numbers, attracted by its message of equality under

---

4. Ibid., 25.

5. Ibid., 28.

the Lord. Operation Mobilization International has created educational centers where Dalit children are given a solid education and learn about Jesus. Literacy and education are important because of the myriad ways that people attempt to scam or confuse the mostly illiterate Dalits, by getting them to sign unfair contracts, for instance.

Many slum dwellers rummage through garbage and wander the streets without shoes. Soles4Souls is an organization that distributes shoes to the slums of Uganda, Venezuela, Ecuador, and many other countries. As is so often the case in cities where the government has failed to provide for the poor, it is religious organizations that seek to identify the pressing needs and that ultimately gain the trust of the people.

The Stakes Are High

Cities and nations that excel in the future will be the ones that have smart governments that can make adjustments and reinvent themselves as the world changes at a rapid pace. Those that can't will be in trouble. The stakes are high. How the world handles urbanization will say a lot about where we are headed in the future.

Cities bring millions of people together, and the synergy results in amazing innovation and the creation of new ways to live. Cities such as Boston and Chennai, India, may produce high-tech inventions that make our world a safer place. Hong Kong and Singapore were able to contain the global SARS outbreak due to their highly educated populations and efficient governments. Portland, Oregon, and Dalian, China, have already demonstrated a heightened sensitivity toward urban planning and the need to be environmentally wise. The best ideas in the twenty-first century will most likely be generated amid the dynamism of cities.

> Cities and nations that excel in the future will reinvent themselves as the world changes at a rapid pace.

Many developed nations will have cities that amass great wealth. They may show us a new way to live—a negative way—in which the wealthy and middle-class are sealed off from the less fortunate to an even greater degree than they are now. While poverty does not necessarily generate violence and terrorism, slums will be breeding grounds for groups looking to overthrow the system in destructive ways. Disease, migration, environmental degradation and conflict could easily make many of the world's cities unlivable.

Christians from wealthy societies will need to resist the temptation to totally separate from the less affluent parts of the city. One word that we would not use to describe Jesus' life and ministry is *safe*. It is vital that churches and missionaries continue to bring Christian hope to the places that the world chooses to ignore. Each of the three types of cities represents tremendous opportunities for evangelism, each in a different way. It is vital that we think strategically about how to approach the urban centers of the twenty-first century. It may be the single most important issue facing Christians in the next one hundred years.

13
a glimpse
of hell

In every sense, North Korea is a failed state.

From birth to adulthood all worshiped Kim Il Sung. There is no other faith so we can't compare it to anything. It was all we knew… If we didn't bow down, we would be killed.

Baek Mi-Jin, North Korean escapee

WHILE CHINA AND India have become the models of emerging nations around the world, the least developed countries remain frighteningly disconnected from the changes that are leading to a higher quality of life for most of the world. Haiti and the Central African Republic are two countries that have suffered greatly from disconnection, having been hampered by corruption, bad government, war, exploitation, and poor geography. These LDC nations are sometimes referred to as "failed states" for their inability to provide for their people. Most LDC nations would love to leave the poverty behind and become successful nations, but geographic, cultural, or other economic factors prevent them.

While most LDC countries crave globalization's interconnectivity and the chance to raise standards of living, one major exception to the rule is North Korea, which has consistently made choices that have resulted in its being the most isolated nation in the world at precisely the moment in history when the world is becoming more interconnected and wealthier than ever before. Within this bizarre state governed by fools and madmen are many Christians, who have not only had to endure grinding poverty but years of abuse and persecution for their faith. In every sense imaginable, North Korea has been a spectacular failure as a country.

After the defeat of Japan in World War II, the nation of Korea was occupied by U.S. forces in the south and Soviet forces in the north. The result was the Korean War, which ended in a stalemate; the war is technically not over even to this day. South Korea, which was poorer than Egypt and most of Africa in the 1950s and 1960s, went on to become a developed nation and a democracy with the world's eleventh largest economy. North Korea became a Stalinist totalitarian dictatorship; after a short period of improvement, it ended up becoming the most depraved, most disconnected, most dysfunctional nation on the planet.

The nation has survived because of its ruthless authoritarianism, its criminal activities, and the personality cult developed by its leader, Kim Il-Sung. When North Korea finally does collapse—and it will—the world will be shocked by the degree of malevolence achieved by the totalitarian regime of the late Kim Il-Sung and his son Kim Jong-il. Imagine the insanity and destructiveness of China's Cultural Revolution lasting *sixty years* instead of ten. That's North Korea today. The stories that eventually emerge from that tragic kingdom will be nothing short of a glimpse of hell.

The Anti-Christ State

Personality cults developed by malevolent leaders such as Mao Zedong and Joseph Stalin are nothing new, but they are destructive. Rarely has a personality cult been started by one leader and successfully passed on to his offspring. But that is what happened in the case of the two Kims that have run North Korea into the ground for the past six decades.

The nation is effectively run as a cult, with the much revered but dead Kim Il-Sung as the "Eternal President." Kim was raised in a Christian home but grew up to not only reject the faith but to make persecution of Christians state policy. His son Kim Jong-Il is just as repressive as his father and lives a life of luxury while his people starve all around him.

The official state ideology is *Juche*, which roughly translated means "self-reliance." As opposed to Christianity, which teaches that we are created by the heavenly Father, Juche teaches that man is the ruler of all things and has the power to decide what he wants. Religion is not necessary. Of course, religion is never eradicated completely in societies. Kim Il-Sung's Juche became a religion in which he plays the part of God and his son Kim Jong-Il takes the role of Jesus. Juche itself is the Spirit. The Trinitarian elements of Father, Son, and Spirit are clearly identifiable in this warped ideology.

The need for a belief in a spiritual father-figure is so great, however, that many North Koreans really do view the Kims as heroic figures—particular the father, Kim Il-Sung. Stories of his goodness and compassion have long inspired North Koreans, who amid the enduring misery of their lives seek something and someone to believe in, no matter how incredulous it seems to outsiders. Stories such as the one of Kim Jong-Il's scoring three holes-in-one the first time he played a round of golf are taken at face value. Their birthplaces are sacred sites that require pilgrimage by the population. Tales of the Kim Il-Sung humbling himself and handing out bread to the masses circulate the way stories of Jesus do today, inspiring North Koreans to tears.

> **The stories that emerge from that tragic kingdom will be nothing short of a glimpse of hell.**

The reality is that these men have killed and tortured many people at places like Camp 22—a concentration camp the size of Washington, DC. Inside the camps, children are tortured and killed, medical experiments are performed on the people, and starvation is so bad that people eat rats to survive, having reached levels of malnutrition so severe that they lose their sense of taste.

Since the death of Kim Il-Sung in 1994, North Korea has been under the control of Kim Jong-Il. Little is known about this Stalinist state because of its extreme secrecy and detachment from the rest of the world. What is known is that North Korea is a land where even the privileged few struggle to get electricity and enough food to eat. Poverty is extreme. Most of the population is malnourished or starving. Teenagers typically look like elementary school kids, and reports of cannibalism are not unheard of due to frequent famines. Anyone who dares to question the government quickly ends up in one of North Korea's extensive system of prison camps where inmates are tortured and forced to work as slave labor. Within these camps, even newborns are tortured and violently killed. The majority of North Koreans do not know that there is a better world outside: televisions only receive one channel and radios are fixed to one frequency. Nearly two million North Koreans starved to death during the famines of the 1990s, and the country nearly went to war with the United States. I lived in South Korea at the time and remember news reports of the bodies of starved North Koreans floating down the Han River into the South.

Even in today's era of globalization and the openness it brings, Christian persecution abounds in countries like North Korea, Myanmar (Burma), Iran, India, Vietnam, and China. It is a fact that we should never forget. Fortunately, one of the benefits of globalization is that it gets more difficult to hide these kinds of human rights abuses. Whether it's images of prisons available to everyone via Google Earth or images of persecution caught on a cell phone and sent to news agencies, for now, globalization is making it more difficult for oppressive states to get away with persecution. North Korea, however, is so uniquely disconnected from the rest of the world that they are able to get away with more abuses than anyone else. The persecution that Christians have faced in North Korea is particularly grim in that the whole country is one enormous prison. A negative comment about the "Dear Leader" can lead to the execution of an entire family. The main railway line is walled off so that no foreigners can see into the countryside, and most homes have an Orwellian speaker system that allows government propaganda to be played morning to night.[1]

To be a Christian in North Korea is to experience a level of oppression rarely experienced by Christians in the rest of the world. In a book titled *Eyes of the Tailless Animals: Memoirs of a North Korean Woman*, North Korean Christian Soon Ok Lee recounts her hellish experiences within the country's notorious prison system. The Heaven People, as they were called, were especially singled out for abuse. Nevertheless, other prisoners could often sense a hopefulness and spiritual strength among Christians that left them deeply moved.

Fortunately, organizations such as Voice of the Martyrs and Christian Solidarity Worldwide keep a close watch on North Koreans and the persecution they endure. In a shocking yet comprehensive report full of eyewitness testimony, Christian Solidarity Worldwide reported that from a sample of two hundred North Koreans who had defected to the South, 86.5 percent had witnessed a public execution, 64 percent had witnessed the punishment of

---

1. Nicholas Kristoff, "The Hermit Nuclear Kingdom," *New York Review of Books* 52, no 2 (February 10, 2005), http://www.nybooks.com/articles/17721.

an acquaintance for public misconduct, 49 percent had experienced agony over their family background, 38.5 percent had witnessed torture, 92 percent knew about public executions, and 94 percent knew of the existence of prison camps.[2]

A Christian Underground Railroad

In recent years, there have been signs that the regime is struggling. Aside from its constant attempt to blackmail the United States and other countries with nuclear threats (in order to receive a huge pay-off), more and more people are escaping across the border into China, the pro-Kim propaganda is on the wane, bribery is rampant, and an explosion near Kim's train in 2004 appears to have been an assassination attempt. Furthermore, Kim Jong-Il seems to be making sure his financial affairs are in order in case he needs to flee the country. These recent maneuvers combined with troop movements toward the border by the United States and South Korea lead many to believe that a collapse is imminent.[3] As has happened so often in the past, rumors of Kim's impending demise may be premature.

> Globalization makes it more difficult for oppressive states to get away with persecution.

At the same time, news is spreading throughout the country that a Christian underground network has formed that sneaks people out of North Korea and tries to get them to embassies in Vietnam, China, and Thailand, and eventually to freedom in South Korea. This network has been able to take advantage of South Korea's large population of Christians, its geographic location, and the fact that many ethnic Koreans live in China in order to get North Koreans into safe hands. North Koreans are told to look for buildings with crosses on them. An estimated three hundred thousand North Koreans have been smuggled out by this network of Koreans from South Korea, Japan,

---

2. Christian Solidarity Worldwide, *North Korea: A Call to Answer, a Call to Act* (Surrey, UK: Christian Solidarity Worldwide, 2007), 21, http://dynamic.csw.org.uk/article.asp?t=report&id=35

3. Reuben F. Johnson. DPRK on the Verge of Collapse? WorldwideStandard.com, November 26, 2007, http://www.weeklystandard.com/weblogs/TWSFP/2007/11/dprk_on_the_verge_of_collapse.asp.

and the United States. Many non-Christians, including corrupt North Korean officials, are getting into the act as well.

This network, which operates primarily on the border with China, is inspired by the life of Dietrich Bonhoeffer, who resisted the Nazi regime in Germany. Unfortunately, like Bonhoeffer, some of these pastors and missionaries have been arrested and killed for their efforts. Capture can mean death or a fifteen-year sentence in one of North Korea's notorious prisons. Rarely can a prisoner survive more than five years of a sentence. And North Koreans that escape and only make it as far as China may be caught by the Chinese government and sent back, or in the case of women, they may end up becoming sex slaves.

Only forty-one defectors asked for asylum from South Korea in 1995, but in 2006, more than two thousand North Koreans resettled in the South.[4] Amnesty International believes there are up to one hundred thousand living in China, and it is clear that the impact of globalization is making it harder for this malevolent state to continue isolating its suffering people.

Truth and Transition

Technology and trade are also making it more difficult for the North Korean government to keep the truth from its people. More and more people have access to cell phones and are interacting with people from other places as special free-trade economic zones are set up within the country. Many in the country now know that China is a very wealthy country by North Korean standards, and videos of life in wealthy South Korea are being watched by people in secret. But for now, Kim Jong-Il has been able to hang on to power by manipulating other countries, repressing his people, operating criminal networks, and liberalizing just enough to keep the country's economy growing slightly—enough to give some hope and to make the West believe reforms are around the corner.

The regime will eventually collapse, but North Koreans have been so damaged mentally, spiritually, and physically that rebuilding this country into a functional society will take a miracle. It will be a much more difficult transi-

4. Blaine Harden, "As More Take a Chance on Fleeing North Korea, Routes for All Budgets, *Washington Post*, November 18, 2007, http://www.washingtonpost.com/wp-dyn/content/article/2007/11/17/AR2007111701699_pf.html.

tion than Eastern Europe experienced in 1989. The reunification of East and West Germany will seem like a cakewalk compared to the difficulties that will arise if wealthy South Korea attempts to merge quickly with the traumatized, emotionally scarred North. Many of those that have escaped to free countries have been psychologically unable to handle life outside of North Korea.

While globalization can be used for both good and evil, the fact that it relies on openness and empowers people with information and knowledge means that we have more ways to combat oppressive forces and dangers, whether they are of the nature of avian flu, sexual slavery, or a prison-camp nation in East Asia. Christian persecution has not ended, but globalization allows for global mobilization in real time. And while it has not brought an end to the repressive regimes in Burma, Iran, Cuba, and North Korea, it does create a world where the truth within those countries becomes harder to hide.

Technology and trade make it more difficult for the North Korean government to keep the truth from its people.

Meanwhile, we must remember than an estimated four hundred thousand Christians live within North Korea, one hundred thousand of whom are imprisoned in conditions we cannot even begin to imagine. Let us not forget them.

14

a new imperialism
in latin america

Amid prosperity comes the threat of heresy.

*I haven't always been a Christian. I didn't go
to religion to make me happy. I always knew
a bottle of Port would do that. If you want a
religion to make you feel really comfortable,
I certainly don't recommend Christianity.*

C.S. Lewis

MANY OF GLOBALIZATION'S challenges hit the hardest in Latin America. Urbanization, criminal networks, sexual slavery, and a large divide between rich and poor are all realities with which Latin America is contending at the dawn of the twenty-first century. Despite the fact that the region is more prosperous and more democratic than ever, it remains riddled with serious problems. War has ended in El Salvador, but the citizens of that beautiful Central American country are now threatened by transnational gangs. Brazil is now an emerging nation that may become a rich oil nation in the future, but it still treats its black citizens as inferiors. Life for indigenous people in Bolivia and Guatemala remains difficult and poverty-ridden, while Mexico City, Bogotá, Rio De Janeiro, and Lima (and many other cities in the region) have massive slums as a result of the continued flow of immigrants into the city.

Latin America has had a long, bloody history that has left its people disillusioned. In his book *Liberty for Latin America,* Alvaro Vargas Llosa identifies five principles of oppression that have kept the region from succeeding economically: corporatism, state mercantilism, privilege, wealth transfer, and political law. The book makes it clear that numerous cultural and historical factors have come together over the years to keep most Latin American countries from succeeding.

The issues are complex, and even now in an age of unprecedented wealth, only Mexico, Chile, and Brazil show signs of being stable enough to continue as prosperous large-scale economies and emerging nations into the future. Even in countries with the most potential (e.g., Brazil), the wealth remains in the hands of the privileged few while most continue to live in poverty. Issues of race and class continue to plague many Latin American cultures in which the white minority control the vast majority of the wealth.

There have been numerous promises to Latin Americans that better days are ahead. From time to time, dictators have seized control of economic assets and promised to share the wealth with the poorest of the poor. (Hugo Chavez in Venezuela is the latest in a long line of "benevolent" dictators.) At times foreign countries have intervened and tried to impose solutions, promising that their systems would work miracles. Few Americans realize that nearly every country in Latin America has had its government overthrown by the U.S. marines at one point or another over the last 150 years. Through it all, very little has changed and the people remain disillusioned.

The latest group to promise unlimited prosperity to Latin Americans are preachers of the prosperity gospel. This gospel teaches that if you are poor, then you are doing something wrong, and that making money and being rich are signs that God's favor is upon you. Prosperity gospel preachers from America are raking in millions and being televised across the globe from Africa to China. From

Prosperity gospel preachers are being televised around the globe.

elaborate sound-stages and converted sports arenas, they teach that God's preferred method for blessing people is through money. It is a gospel of financial blessings and well-being. Using Bible verses taken out of context and generally Christian concepts devoid of theological content, they teach people that "victory in Jesus" means total happiness now in this life. Christ's redeeming work is not about his restoration of creation through the forgiveness of sins, but rather it is a self-help program that is guaranteed to work—if you give your money.

While not all of these preachers demand money on television, they market themselves extensively with books, CDs, and videos that spend more time talking about empowerment for your own self-betterment than dealing with issues of sin, repentance, and self-denial. Whereas Jesus' ministry began with an emphatic message for all to repent (see Mark 1:15 and Matt 4:17), the prosperity gospel avoids anything that sounds so judgmental. More than a few of these preachers exclaim that they want to stay positive so that non-Christians will give the gospel a chance. But what could be more positive than being saved from sin and restored to full communion with God? For the prosperity preachers, this message is too negative; they cater to people's religious hang-ups about sin and judgment instead of preaching Jesus' message of freedom from bondage. Jesus' redemptive work is not enough for the prosperity preachers, who are more interested in talking about how God can bless you materially right now. The *self*-centered nature of their sermons gives away the fact that they spend little time thinking about who Jesus actually was and what he did.

The Americanization of the Gospel

This points to a larger problem, namely, the Americanization of the gospel. The United States is the richest, most powerful nation that has ever existed in the history of the planet. To think that America's wealth and power do not affect our theology is ludicrous and self-delusional. All people from any culture can be transformed by the gospel, but our cultures can easily transform our local Christianity into something that is less than biblical. The prosperity gospel could only originate in a culture that is relatively free from suffering and persecution and that has an economic system supported by multiple safeguards, including the rule of law and strong governing branches, that enable upward mobility.

In other words, the prosperity gospel is the product of a culture that is so wealthy it can hardly relate to the agrarian societies portrayed in the Bible stories—stories filled with persecution, famine, war, locusts, refugees, and untrustworthy government. As we saw in chapters 1 and 2, for most of human history, the people of the world have been very poor. By current standards, the poverty in Jesus' time was truly appalling, yet Jesus consistently preaches against the love of money throughout the Gospels. If Jesus, in his poor, impoverished land two thousand years ago, felt the need, again and again, to preach against trusting in material possessions, what on earth would he say to us today? Jesus would not be preaching the message transmitted via satellite around the world by preachers of the prosperity gospel.

Most Christians throughout human history have not had the luxury of sitting around trying to attain happiness and prosperity. Their lives have been marked by persecution, disease, poverty, and war. To Christians living in developed nations today, the fallen nature of the world is not as painfully obvious and constantly present in their daily lives as it has been to most Christians throughout history. Only in an age where very few of us have to endure significant hardship can Christianity's message of freedom from sin be deemed "not enough" by people claiming to follow Christ. Apparently, the victory of Christ must be tied to immediate financial and emotional gains or else it is not a victory worth preaching about.

The cross is rarely seen or preached about either. In the prosperity gospel, Jesus does not ask us to take up our cross, because he has already done it for us. We are not called to take on the burden of being "in this world but not of this world," because with the prosperity gospel, we can have both. Jesus said, "Whoever wants to save his life will lose it, but whoever loses his life for me will find it. What good will it be for a man if he gains the whole world, yet forfeits his soul?" (Matt 16:25–26). Preachers of the prosperity gospel do not seem to realize that for Jesus there is a difference between self-empowerment and self*less* empowerment.

Not only is the assumption that God wants all of us Christians to be rich heretical, but it is also terribly presumptuous in that it assumes that we Christians would be able to handle the wealth given to us. All of us, at times, have struggled with the power that money has over us, and most of us have very little of it. Our churches often split over money, as do our marriages. Are we to believe that God's purpose for us on earth is to live in financial abundance and that this will somehow empower us to be servants walking in the footsteps of Christ? Very few of us have that kind of spiritual maturity. To say that God wants us all to be rich makes about as much sense as saying that God wants every man to be sexually irresistible to all the women he meets (of course, the man wouldn't act on it, being the good Christian that he is). After all, God likes beautiful things, and symmetrical faces are more attractive than nonsymmetrical faces.

The reality is that money, like sex, like security, like power, is something that we humans, Christians included, struggle with in this life, and money tempts us to walk away from trusting Jesus, just as the rich young ruler did in Luke 18. Greed for mammon is a dangerous temptation, and the idea that ministries would encourage people to yield to that temptation is sickening.

American Christianity, influenced by the capitalism that has brought it untold wealth, has a very transactional quality to it. "I give you something (my faith), God, so you must give me something back." For the purveyors of the prosperity gospel, blessings are not for the humble, who stand in awe of their salvation, to be dispensed in the way the Almighty sees fit; rather, blessings are tangible goods that prove that our transaction with God has gone through. Blessings are the sound of the credit card being accepted after God-the-cashier has swiped it.

Jesus would not be preaching the prosperity gospel.

We've had faith, we've given the money, and now we reap the benefits. The need in American Christianity for *proven success*, *a predictable formula that works*, and for *instant gratification* is reminiscent of the American desires that have propelled us to pursue life, liberty, and happiness through commerce for more than two hundred years. These traits have helped us build an American empire, but they will not help us expand the kingdom of God, and it is to the latter to which we are called.

Although the world has been getting wealthier overall due to the latest round of hyperglobalization, nearly a billion people still make under one dollar a day. Sadly, many throughout Latin America (and other places as well, particularly South Korea) are being fed a Western theology that seems diametrically opposed to Jesus' teachings, which persistently warn of the danger of mammon. This new theological imperialism is reaching many new believers in poverty-stricken nations and making false promises in the name of Jesus Christ. In Brazil, Costa Rica, Nicaragua and places far beyond Latin America, this heretical gospel is gaining momentum.

The prosperity gospel is particularly dangerous because it seems so plausible in cultures where religion is already one of pragmatic transactions with the gods. Ironically, this new heretical prosperity Christianity simply substitutes one poor god for another poor god—one god of appeasement and blessing for another. Consequently, this American prosperity gospel not only offers false material hope to the poor in least developed nations and emerging nations, but it ultimately disconnects them spiritually from the Jesus of the Bible, who knows them and knows their pain and suffering as well. The belief being propagated across the world's poorest lands is that the closer you are to God, the more you will look like a rich Westerner. Nothing could be further from the truth.

For Jesus and for many Christians in the world today, the prayer to "give us this day our daily bread" is meant literally. It is not just a polite acknowledgment that God gives us food; it is a plea for God to provide enough to sustain us for one more day. Despite the difficult conditions that they face, our persecuted Christian brothers and sisters radiate a joy born of total dependence on God to provide for their needs. It is the freedom of spiritual and physical poverty.

The best thing that could happen to most American televangelists would be to spend a year living in the Democratic Republic of Congo. These preachers seem to have no sense that greater, more real things can come into focus when we are free of excessive materialism and security. Behind the prosperity gospel is an assumption that God can easily be defined and his behavior predicted with absolute certainty: To know God means to know him completely, with no surprises, no mystery, and ultimately no need for much faith. This God simply acts in predictable ways for those who know him, and if he doesn't, it is *your* problem. It reduces blessings down to a science and makes God nothing more than a fat Buddha who will give you money if you rub his belly correctly.

> For many Christians in the world today, the prayer to "give us this day our daily bread" is meant literally.

The prosperity gospel reveals not only a shallow understanding of scripture and how to interpret it but also a very limited (and, ironically, poor) vision of what God truly wants in our lives. When we are truly in touch with our own sinfulness and genuinely repent, we will find that we do not have the audacity to spend time pinning our hopes on material wealth for we are so grateful that we have been saved from our own evil.

Globalization and Mammon

With the wealth generated by globalization and the global reach enabled by technology, we should not be surprised if benign-looking forms of Christianity emerge that are extremely popular and heretical. As this book has argued, globalization is not controlled by any one person or organization. Nations, companies, and people acting in self-interest look beyond their borders and look for ideas, products, jobs, and faith. It is not a process we should discourage, for it is natural and will ultimately lead to many good things.

While there seems to be very little critical reflection in the prosperity gospel movement, it at least provides the opportunity for those of us Christians outside of the movement to remember that the way to Christ always involves the way of the cross daily. Millions have probably been encouraged or helped by these prosperity preachers—products of globalization—but that is a sign of God's grace, not of the spiritual and theological content of their message. Even if the preacher is full of smiles and is sincere, a gospel preached that omits self-denial and sacrifice is dangerous to our souls. Christ's invitation to the lepers, the prostitutes, and the destitute was not about inviting them into the kingdom of financial wealth or even the kingdom of globalization, for those kingdoms are far too shallow and limited. Instead Jesus and the Bible promise a kingdom that is so great that the word *gold* is only used as a limited metaphor for the riches to come.

appendix

7 Important Questions Regarding Globalization

WE NOW LIVE in a world of greater freedom, more democracy, a higher quality of life, and less war than ever before in human history. Much of this is due to a phenomenon known as globalization. In light of the many changes that are occurring in our world and the fact that we are currently in an era of unprecedented Christian growth, it is helpful to take a closer look at what globalization means for all of us. Here are seven of the most commonly asked questions regarding globalization:

1. **What is globalization?** There is no precise definition of globalization. In general, it refers to an accelerated interconnecting of the world's economic, cultural, technological, and political spheres. Companies like Wal-Mart are no longer tied to consumers in one country, but rather they position themselves to be everywhere at all times. Hip-hop inner-city music becomes the style for youth around the world, from Harlem to Tokyo to Tel Aviv. The Internet allows people from all over the world to meet and exchange everything from stock tips to bomb-making instructions. And new political and economic entities, such as the World Trade Organization, coordinate economic policy for much of the world. In other words, at every level, our world is becoming interdependent. Nations do not stand alone. They are constantly interacting with each other at every level of human society.

2. **Has globalization happened before?** To some extent, globalization is always occurring. Since the beginning of time, the peoples of the world have interacted and traded. There have been two previous eras of what I call hyperglobalization, periods in which the world experienced massive

technological and economic shifts. The first era (c. 1492 to c. 1648) was ushered in by Christopher Columbus and the age of discovery. Inventions such as the compass, clipper ship, gunpowder, and printing press all came together to enable a new era of massive global trade, and ultimately catastrophic wars. The second era (c. 1830 to 1917) saw the Industrial Revolution introduce mass factories, machinery, steam-powered ships and trains, as well as the automobile and the airplane. This period ended with two world wars. Our current era of hyperglobalization began with the end of the cold war and the shrinking of the microchip, which opened up doors to new levels of global trade and technological innovation. As former socialist countries India and China turn to free-market capitalism, they alone are responsible for adding more than two billion new workers to the global marketplace.

3. **Is *globalization* a dirty word?** No. Like democracy, globalization is value-neutral. (The Nazi party came to power under a democracy, and today, Iran's irresponsible government is a democracy.) *How* the processes of globalization are used determines whether it is good or bad. When my American friend opens up a factory in China and demands that the employees be paid decently and treated well (and introduced to Christianity), then globalization is working well. He makes money, American consumers get a less expensive product (saving themselves money), and Chinese workers get a job in a safe place and learn about Christianity. But when a Romanian girl is kidnapped by the Russian mafia and transported to brothels in Israel and Mexico before eventually being smuggled across the U.S. border, globalization is providing opportunities for evil.

4. **Do the rich get richer and the poor get poorer?** No. This is a common misconception. The rich get richer, but the poor get richer as well. In chapter 7, I mention that Vietnam has seen poverty decrease from 51 percent of the population to 8 percent. Free trade brings down prices, which allows the poor to buy more with what little they have, raising their standard of living. Free trade also brings more job opportunities. Furthermore, our recent period of globalization has led to lower mortality rates, lower unemployment levels, higher nutrition levels, a massive decrease in disease, and fewer wars than at any time in history. So, to say that the

rich get richer and the poor get poorer flies in the face of two hundred years of economic history.

The challenge that does emerge is this: The *gap* between rich and poor becomes greater. The wealthiest people suddenly become far wealthier than the poorest people. There were only a handful of billionaires twenty years ago. In 2007, there were 946 billionaires, and that figure is currently growing by 19 percent each year. Many of them are in places as unlikely as Kazakhstan and Azerbaijan. While cell phones in Africa can undoubtedly create a better quality of life and higher income levels for the average African, a much smaller percentage of the global population will see their net worth grow exponentially. Even wealthy countries like Japan will have to deal with a new divide between their richest and poorest citizens. So, despite the fact that developing nations like Vietnam and Kazakhstan, as well as high-tech nations such as the United States and Japan, will see their overall quality of life improve, it will often feel very unfair.

5. Does globalization mean I will lose my job? It's possible. Globalization gives both employees and employers more opportunities. It is highly unlikely that your company will move your job to a country like China. But if it does, the Chinese cannot rest easy either, because that new job might be moved to Bangladesh two years later. Your auto plant in Indiana may move to Mexico, but the Japanese and Chinese will open up an auto plant in Alabama and Ohio. And even if the clothes you wear are labeled "Made in China," they may actually have been made in Cambodia for an American company. (Eighty percent of the profits made in China go to overseas companies). Even more confusing is the fact that many products are no longer made in one location, so targeting particular nations as the source of job loss makes less and less sense. In other words, all jobs and all businesses are now deeply interlinked.

Every country, from wealthy Finland to poorer Uruguay, has to learn to be more flexible. Workers in the first world (developed nations) will have to be more educated and increasingly will need to have more unique skills in order to compete. And workers in the third world (least developed countries) will have to perform at higher standards than they have in the past. Politicians will increasingly blame other countries and encourage trade wars to stop "the loss of jobs," but this will only result in higher prices and fewer opportunities for the people they represent. The bottom line is that the price for a safer world with more people employed overall is a very high rate of competition and a lack of job security.

6. Can globalization be stopped? Globalization is not controlled by any one country or by a secret club of wealthy businessmen. It is a movement from the ground up driven by technology and communication. Inevitably, the change it brings is so great that politicians seek to slow it down. In previous eras, globalization has led to massive conflict and the rise of new dangerous ideologies. It could be that al Qaeda's brand of Islamic fascism will serve as a counteraction to globalization. Perhaps a new form of communism will arise to defend the workers. Or it is possible that as emerging nations like China and India become world powers, they will miscalculate and start a war with their neighbors.

7. What does globalization mean for missions? It means opportunity and challenge. Christianity is entering many formerly closed countries. Christian materials can be stored on memory sticks, CDs, and pocket computers, and easily taken across borders. Missionaries can communicate with their families back home for free over the Internet. And the face of Christianity and missions will be less and less Western as workers from throughout the world join us in the Great Commission. Furthermore, the radical changes that most societies are undergoing open the door to evangelism like little else. Contrary to popular belief, eras of rapid technological change lead to *more* religious growth, not less.

In the long run (and for many in the short term as well), globalization will make the world a better place. But there will be moments of painful adjustment and heightened tensions. The spirit of mammon and greed will be alive and well. There will be the temptation for the rich to disconnect from the poor. We will be encouraged by politicians to hate our "enemies" and view people as competitors. All of these things could potentially infect the church.

In addition to these things, because the speed and scale of globalization is unprecedented, issues like sexual slavery, transnational terrorism, illegal immigration, refugee crises, questionable medical procedures, stock market meltdowns, and environmental degradation and air pollution will pose greater threats than ever before. In each case, there is much that we can do as Christians. We will need to resist the greed and covetousness that the global market will encourage and tackle the difficult issues that others will be happy to ignore.

Jesus lived in a premodern age. It was a time in which children died early deaths, diseases decimated populations, and ignorance stifled opportunities. I believe God has no objection to the fact that human innovation has ushered in an age of greater wealth and higher standards of living through greater cross-cultural interaction. He is the creator of our brains and our diversity after all. In the long run, we will see humankind make another dramatic advance in living standards over the next fifty years. As always, there will be sin and tragedy also. Our job is not to simplistically condemn globalization as others gain privileges that our society has benefited from for a long time but to make sure that amid all the change, we stand firm as the salt of the earth representing the one who is "the Alpha and Omega, the First and the Last, the Beginning and the End" (Rev 22:13).

index

corruption, 14, 36, 39, 53, 59, 90, 95, 96, 116
creation care, 86
Crichton, Michael, 81
crime syndicates, 3, 4, 38, 68, 69, 70, 76, 90
Defense Advanced Research Projects Agency, 84
deforestation, 87
democracy: conditions for, 89
developed nations: definition of, 13; fiscal irresponsibility of, 23
divide between rich and poor. See under prosperity
Dubai. See United Arab Emirates
Easterly, William, 36–37
East Kazakhstan State University, 59
economic dependence: and conflict, 18
education, 57–60; and literacy, 108; online, 57; role of English, 58; and terrorism, 78; training in ethics, 58–60. See also universities
Egypt, 14, 21, 107; slums, 106, 107
emerging nations: birthrates in, 28; definition of, 12; economic output of, 28
End of Medicine, The, 17
End of Poverty, The, 35
energy: alternative sources, 85; conservation, 85; and emerging nations, 85; oil, 83
environmental issues, 81–88; Christian response, 86–88; and consumerism, 83, 84; pollution, 82, 83; solutions, 82, 84–86
environmental refugees, 83
ethics, training in. See education: training in ethics
Ethiopia: famine, 36; foreign investment, 22; slums, 106
Europe: Christianity in, 51–56; core values, 56; distrust of religion, 53; immigrant Christianity, 54–55; re-Christianization of, 55; and secular-

ism, 52, 53, 54, 56; spirituality in, 54. See also country names
European Union, 19
Evangelical Environmental Network, 86
evangelism: opportunities for, 20, 130; role of business in, 40; in Russia, 94–96; and urbanization, 109; and Western missionaries, 48
failed states, 111
Finding, Deborah, 69
first world: definition of, 12
fishery depletion, 86
Floresta, 87
foreign aid, 35. See also antipoverty efforts
foreign investment, 14, 19, 31. See also under China
France, 51–52
Gates, Bill, 33
George, Nathan, 41
Ghana, 14, 67
global cooling, 2, 81
globalization: and competition, 55; definition of, 127; effect on social services, 55; fears of, 21, 23, 33; frequent questions about, 127; goodwill toward, 32; in history, 127; and human rights, 24; and interconnectivity, 17, 18, 19; and job loss, 129 (See also outsourcing; off-shoring); and literacy, 57; and missions, 130; and openness, 17, 19–20, 117; and perception, 21; and persecution, 114; and religion, 61; and technology, 23; and turmoil, 21; and war, 79, 130; value neutral, 125, 128. See also terrorism; prosperity
Global South, 12
global warming, 2, 81
God TV, 46
gospel: Americanization of, 121
Grameen Bank, 38
Greenfaith, 86
history: turning points in, 9, 10, 12